Maps Globes Graphs

Level E

Writer
Henry Billings

Consultants

Marian Gregory
Teacher
San Luis Coastal Unified School District
San Luis Obispo, California

Gloria Sesso
Supervisor of Social Studies
Half Hollow Hills School District
Dix Hills, New York

Norman McRae, Ph.D.
Former Director of Fine Arts and Social
Studies
Detroit Public Schools
Detroit, Michigan

Edna Whitfield
Former Social Studies Supervisor
St. Louis Public Schools
St. Louis, Missouri

Marilyn Nebenzahl
Social Studies Consultant
San Francisco, California

Karen Wiggins
Director of Social Studies
Richardson Independent School District
Richardson, Texas

Check the Maps•Globes•Graphs Website to find more fun geography activities at home.

Go to www.HarcourtAchieve.com/mggwelcome.html

Harcourt Achieve
Rigby • Steck-Vaughn

www.HarcourtAchieve.com
1.800.531.5015

Acknowledgments

Cartography

Land Registration and Information Service
Amherst, Nova Scotia, Canada

Gary J. Robinson

MapQuest.com, Inc.

R.R. Donnelley and Sons Company

XNR Productions Inc., Madison, Wisconsin

Photography Credits

COVER (globe, clouds): ©PhotoDisc; p. 4 ©Superstock; pp. 5, 6, 7(b) ©PhotoDisc; p. 7(a) ©Zuckerman/ PhotoEdit

Illustration Credits

Dennis Harms pp. 8, 56, 64, 70, 71, 72, 75; Michael Krone pp. 22, 86, 87; T.K. Riddle pp. 88, 89; Rusty Kaim p. 4

ISBN 0-7398-9105-7

Contents

Geography Themes

In *Maps•Globes•Graphs* you will learn about some of the tools that scientists use to study **geography**. Geography is the study of Earth, its features, and the ways people live and work on Earth. There are five **themes**, or main topics, to help people organize ideas as they study geography.

The Five Themes of Geography
- **Location**
- **Place**
- **Human/Environment Interaction**
- **Movement**
- **Regions**

Location

Location describes where something is found. You can name a location by using its address. Another way you can tell the location of something is by describing what it is near or what is around it. Location helps us learn where a certain lake is found, or how far a person from Maine must travel to get to Idaho.

 Look at this photograph. How would you describe the location of this home?

_____

_____

Place

Place describes the kinds of features that make a location different from any other on Earth. **Physical features** are part of the natural environment. Some physical features are bodies of water, landforms, climate, soil, and plants and animals. **Human features** are developed or made by people. These features can include airports, buildings, highways, businesses, parks, and playgrounds.

The city in this photograph is Minneapolis, Minnesota. As you study the picture, look for physical and human features of Minneapolis.

 Use the physical and human features you find in the photograph and describe Minneapolis, Minnesota.

_____

_____

_____

Human/Environment Interaction

Human/Environment Interaction describes how people affect the environment and how the environment affects people. This theme also explains how people depend on the environment. For example, people depend on the land for good soil to grow crops.

Human/Environment Interaction demonstrates how people adapt to their environment. It explains how people make changes to live in their surroundings.

 How do the people in these photographs adapt to the change of seasons in their climate?

_____

_____

_____

Human/Environment Interaction also considers how people change the environment to meet their needs and wants. Sometimes people change the course of a river to uncover flooded land or to bring water where it is needed.

 Look at the photograph of the dam shown here. How do you think changing the flow of a river's water might affect the plants and animals in the area?

_____

_____

_____

Movement

Movement explains how people, goods, information, and ideas move from place to place. The movement of people from other countries to settle in the United States is one example of movement. Another example is trade. Goods move across the country or around the world through trade. The spread of information and ideas through the Internet is another kind of movement.

Name two ways that people, goods, information, and ideas move from place to place.

_____

_____

_____

Both photographs above show movement. On the line below each picture write **People/Goods** if the picture shows movement of people and goods. Write **Information/Ideas** if the picture shows movement of information and ideas.

Regions

Regions name areas that share one or more features. Physical features, such as landforms, natural resources, or climate can describe regions. Appalachia is a region in the eastern part of the United States defined by its physical feature— the Appalachian Mountains. Human features, such as land use, politics, religion, or language can also describe regions. Regions can be large or small.

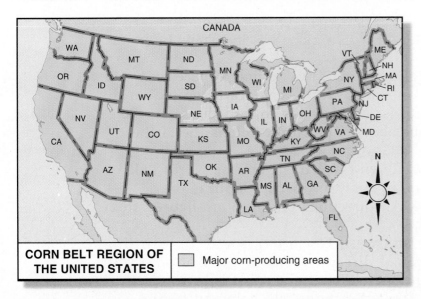

CORN BELT REGION OF THE UNITED STATES

Major corn-producing areas

 Look at the map of the United States shown here. List the states that make up the Corn Belt. What makes the Corn Belt a region?

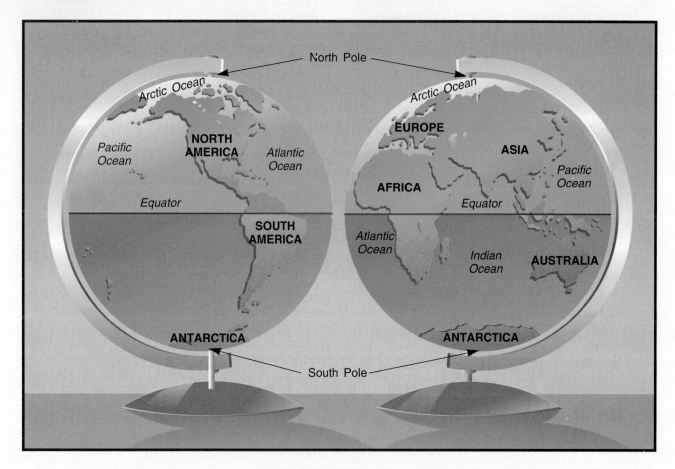

A globe is a model of Earth. Like Earth, a globe has the shape of a sphere, or ball.

The drawing above shows a globe. How can you find a place on the globe? One way is to know its direction. North America is located on the northern part of the globe. North is the direction toward the North Pole. Find the North Pole on the globe above. The **North Pole** is the farthest point north on Earth.

The South Pole is at the opposite end of Earth from the North Pole. The **South Pole** is the farthest point south on Earth. South is the direction toward the South Pole. All directions on Earth are figured from the North and South Poles.

Two other directions are east and west. North (N), south (S), east (E), and west (W) are called the **cardinal directions.** You know that once you are facing north, then east is always to your right. West is to your left. South is behind you. Knowing these directions will help you to find places. Practice using directions on the map above.

► South America is which direction from North America?

► The Arctic Ocean is which direction from North America?

► The Pacific Ocean is which direction from North and South America?

► The Atlantic Ocean is which direction from North and South America?

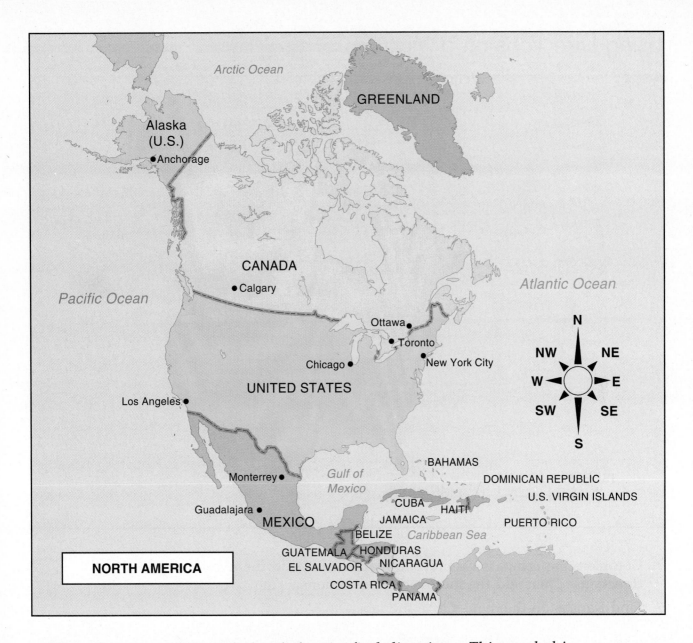

Maps have a special symbol to help you find directions. This symbol is called a **compass rose**. Look at the map above. Find the compass rose. North (N), south (S), east (E), and west (W) are all marked on the compass rose.

There are also other directions on the compass rose. These directions are in between the cardinal directions. They are called **intermediate directions**. The intermediate directions are northeast (NE), southeast (SE), northwest (NW), and southwest (SW). You need these to locate places that are between the cardinal directions

Find Chicago on the map. Find Toronto. What direction is Toronto from Chicago? It is between north and east, or northeast.

► Find Calgary on the map of North America above. In which direction would you travel from Calgary to reach Anchorage?

► From Monterrey, what direction is Guadalajara?

► From Los Angeles, what direction is Monterrey?

Using Directions on a Map

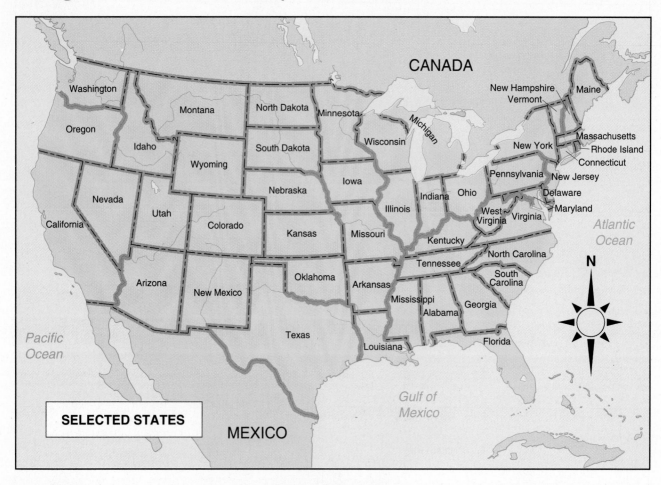

1. Complete the compass rose on the map above. Add the missing cardinal directions. Then add the intermediate directions.

2. Find Kansas on the map. Circle the label.

   a. Which state is north of Kansas? _____

   b. Which state is south of Kansas? _____

   c. Which state is east of Kansas? _____

   d. Which state is west of Kansas? _____

3. Which state is northeast of Utah? _____

4. Which state is southeast of Arkansas? _____

5. Which state is southwest of Illinois? _____

6. Which state is northwest of Iowa? _____

7. What is west of California? _____

8. What is southeast of Texas? _____

Using Directions on a Map

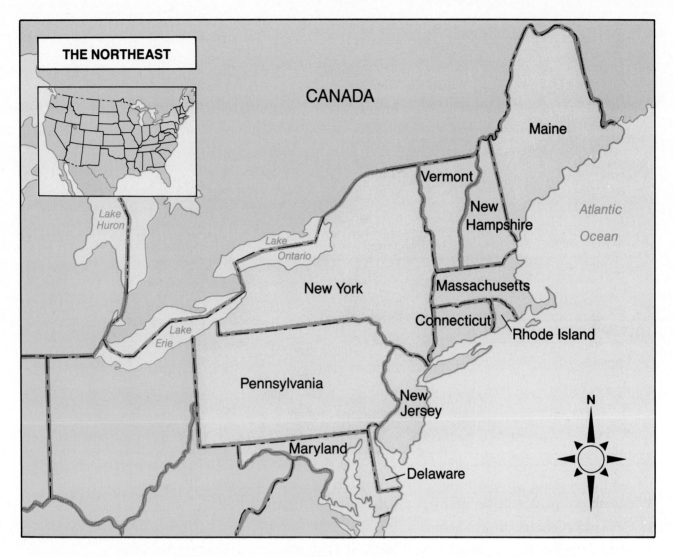

1. Complete the compass rose. First add the cardinal directions. Then add the intermediate directions.

2. Write a direction to make each sentence true.

   a. New Hampshire is _____ of Massachusetts.

   b. Pennsylvania is _____ of New York.

   c. New Jersey is _____ of Connecticut.

   d. New Hampshire is _____ of Rhode Island.

   e. Maine is _____ of New Hampshire.

3. Draw a conclusion. Find the small map of the United States above. It shows where the Northeast region of the United States is located. Why do you think this region is called the Northeast?

   _____

Using Directions on a Map

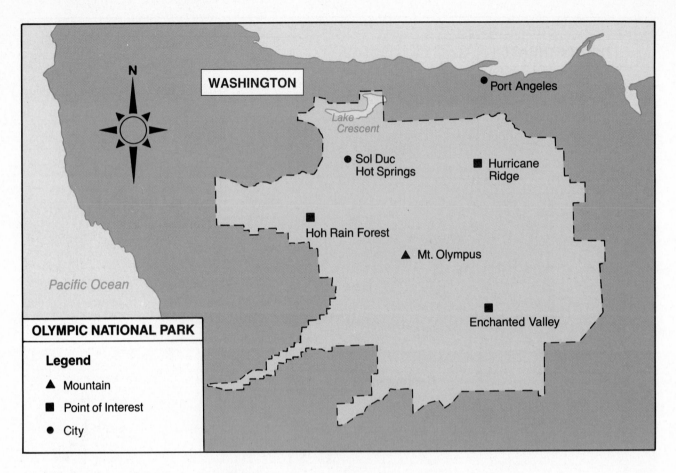

You are going on a camping trip through Olympic National Park in Washington. You will be hiking and do not want to get lost.

1. Complete the compass rose.
2. Your trip begins at Hurricane Ridge. It is in the northeast part of the park. Circle it on your map.

   What direction would you look to see Mt. Olympus? _____
3. You will hike to Lake Crescent from Hurricane Ridge. What direction

   will you be walking? _____
4. From Lake Crescent you will hike to Sol Duc Hot Springs. What

   direction will you be going? _____
5. You want to camp in the Hoh Rain Forest. What direction do you hike

   from Sol Duc Hot Springs to the Hoh Rain Forest? _____
6. What direction is the Pacific Ocean from the Hoh Rain Forest? _____
7. Your last stop will be at the Enchanted Valley. It is in the southeastern part of the park. What direction will you travel to get back to

   Hurricane Ridge from the Enchanted Valley? _____

Skill Check

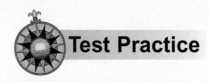

Vocabulary Check   compass rose   North Pole   intermediate directions
                      cardinal directions South Pole

Choose from the words above to make each sentence true.

1. North, south, east, and west are the _____ .

2. Directions on Earth are figured from the _____

   and the _____ .

3. Northwest and southeast are two of the _____ .

Map Check

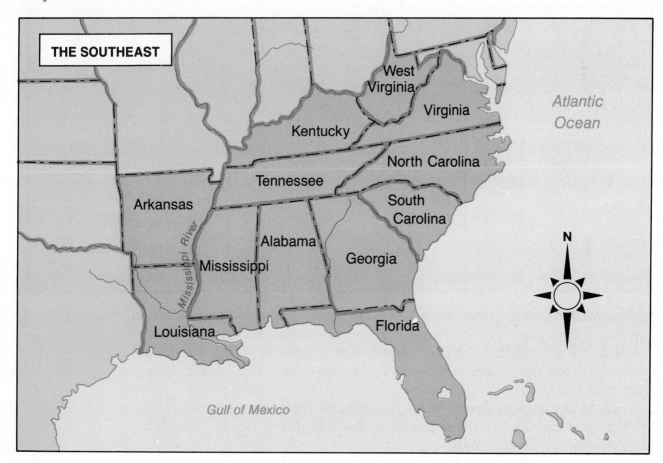

THE SOUTHEAST

West Virginia

Virginia

Kentucky

Atlantic Ocean

North Carolina

Tennessee

Arkansas

South Carolina

Mississippi River

Alabama

Mississippi

Georgia

Louisiana

Florida

N

Gulf of Mexico

1. What state is southwest of South Carolina? _____

2. What state is northeast of Kentucky? _____

3. What direction is North Carolina from Tennessee? _____

4. What two states are west of the Mississippi River? _____

   and _____

2 Symbols and Legends

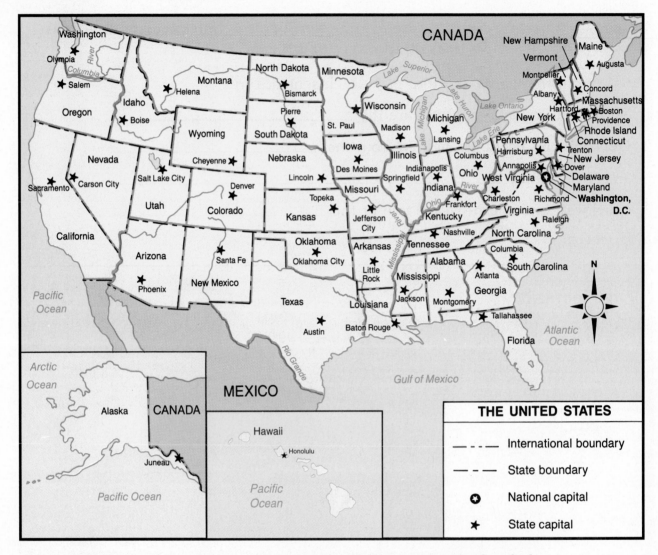

A **symbol** on a map represents something that is on Earth. Symbols can stand for cities, or mountains, or natural resources. To find the meaning of a symbol, read the legend. The **legend** explains what every symbol on the map means. We use the symbols and the legend to learn from the map.

Look at the legend above. Find the symbol for a state boundary. A **state boundary** shows where one state ends and another begins. Find a state boundary on the map.

Find the symbol for an international boundary in the legend. An **international boundary** shows where one country ends and another begins.

► Find your state on the map. What is the state capital? What states border your state? What are their capitals?

► Does your state have an international boundary? If so, what country shares a border with your state?

► What countries border the United States?

POLITICAL MAP OF MEXICO

- – ‑ – International boundary
- – – State boundary
- ⊗ National capital

Some maps show special information about a place. Political maps show the boundaries separating states and countries. Other maps may show yearly rainfall or where people live. That is why the title is so important. The **title** tells you the purpose of the map.

Look at the title of the map above. It is a **political map** of Mexico. What can you expect to learn from this map? You can expect to find capital cities and state and international boundaries. The country of Mexico has 31 states. Like the United States, it has a national capital. Find the symbol for a national capital on this map and on the map on page 14.

► What city is the national capital of the United States?

► What city is the national capital of Mexico?

► What country touches the northern international boundary of Mexico?

► Name two Mexican states along this boundary.

Reading a Political Map

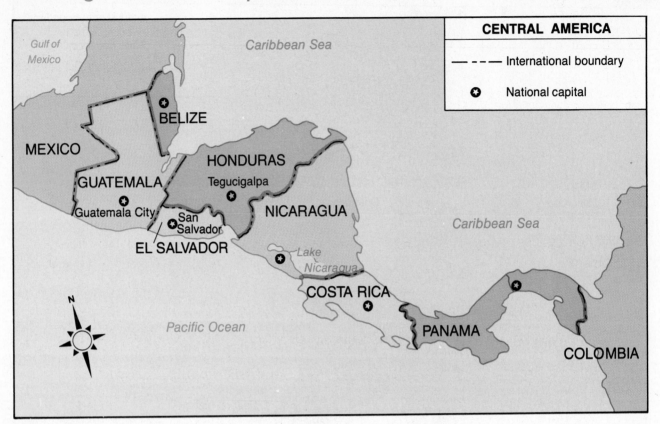

MAP ATTACK!

- **Read the title.** This map shows _____.
- **Read the legend.** Check (✔) each symbol after you read its meaning. Check (✔) a matching symbol on the map.
- **Read the compass rose.** Circle the four cardinal directions. Label the intermediate directions.

1. Does this map show states or countries? _____

   How do you know? _____
2. Trace the borders of Costa Rica in red. What countries share a

   border with Costa Rica? _____
3. Write the capital city of each of these countries on the map where it belongs.

   Panama City, Panama   San Jose, Costa Rica
   Managua, Nicaragua   Belmopan, Belize
4. Draw a conclusion. What countries have coastlines on both the Caribbean Sea and the Pacific Ocean?

_____

Reading a Political Map

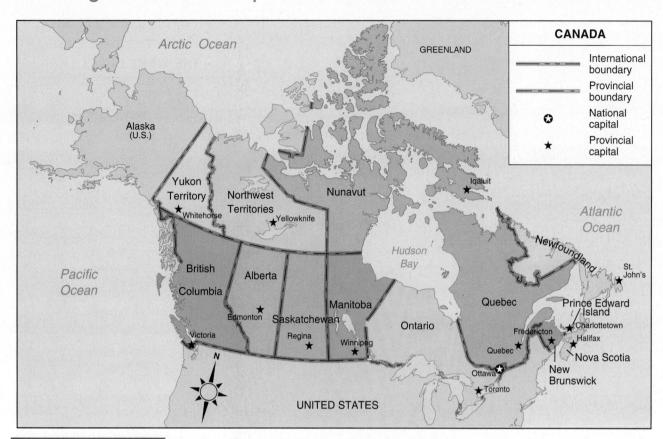

MAP ATTACK!

Follow the steps on page 16 to begin reading this map.

1. Canada is divided into ten provinces and three territories. The border lines look like state borders. Why is the border different between

   the Yukon Territory and Alaska? _____

2. Circle the capital city of Saskatchewan. Write its name.

   _____

3. Trace the borders of Saskatchewan in red.

   Which province is west of Saskatchewan? _____

   Which province is east of Saskatchewan? _____

4. What is the national capital of Canada? _____

5. Halifax is the capital of _____ .

6. Iqaluit is the capital of _____

7. What is the capital of the Northwest Territories? _____

8. What is the capital of the Yukon Territory? _____

Reading a Political Map

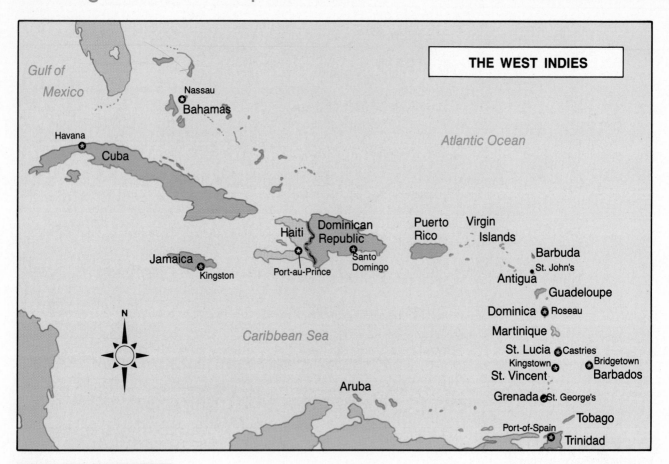

MAP ATTACK!

Follow the steps on page 16 to begin reading this map.

1. Find the island that is divided into two separate countries. Name each country and its capital.

    a. _____

    b. _____

2. Locate the Bahamas on the map above. Nassau is the capital city of the Bahamas. Draw a line south from Nassau to the bottom of the map.

    What countries do you cross? _____

3. Write the intermediate direction that makes each sentence true.

    a. Martinique is _____ of Barbados.

    b. Trinidad and Tobago are _____ of Puerto Rico.

    c. Guadeloupe is _____ of Aruba.

4. Draw a conclusion. The West Indies form the northern and eastern

    boundary of what sea? _____

Skill Check

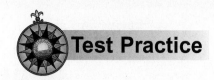

Vocabulary Check   symbol   legend   title
                        boundaries   political map

Use each word or phrase to finish a sentence.

1. A _____ shows the boundaries that separate different states or countries.

2. The map _____ tells you what the map is about.

3. Lines that separate states or countries are _____.

4. The _____ tells you what the symbols on a map mean.

5. A _____ on a map can stand for a city, a mountain, or a resource.

Map Check

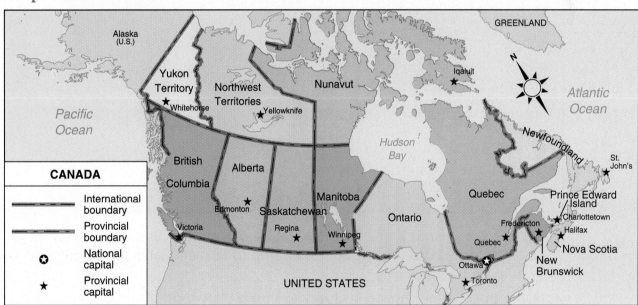

Match the capital with the province.

1. _____ Toronto   A. Manitoba

2. _____ Edmonton   B. Ontario

3. _____ Winnipeg   C. Quebec

4. _____ Quebec   D. Nova Scotia

5. _____ Victoria   E. Alberta

6. _____ Halifax   F. British Columbia

Geography Themes Up Close

Place is a location that has physical and human features that set it apart from other locations. Physical features can include bodies of water, landforms, climate, and plants and animals. Human features can include the kind of government, customs, art, buildings, and other things made by people. The map below shows Florida and some of its features.

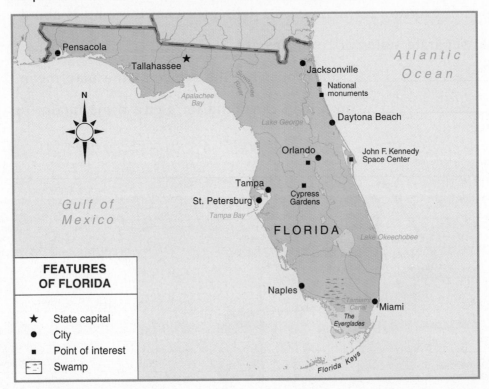

1. Big Cypress Swamp is one physical feature of Florida. This swamp is east of Naples, Florida. Use the symbol for swamp to find and label Big Cypress Swamp on the map.

2. Name three other physical features of Florida shown on the map.

_____

_____

_____

3. The John F. Kennedy Space Center was set up in 1964 as a launch site for space missions. It is on the coast southeast of Daytona Beach. Circle this feature on the map. Then, mark **P** next to the circle if it is a physical feature. Mark **H** if it is a human feature.

4. Walt Disney World, near Orlando, is a human feature of Florida. Use the Point of Interest symbol in the legend to find Walt Disney World. Then, label it on the map.

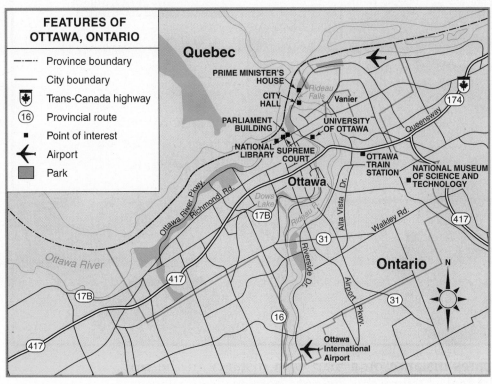

FEATURES OF OTTAWA, ONTARIO

Legend:
- – · – · – Province boundary
- —— City boundary
- 🍁 Trans-Canada highway
- (16) Provincial route
- ■ Point of interest
- ← Airport
- ▨ Park

5. The Ottawa River forms the northwestern border of Ottawa. Label the Ottawa River. Then, mark **P** next to your label if it is a physical feature. Mark **H** if it is a human feature.

6. Name two physical features of Ottawa. _____

_____

7. The Rockcliffe Airport is a human feature in the northeast corner of Ottawa. Use the airport symbol in the legend to find Rockcliff Airport. Then, label it on the map.

8. What are two other human features of Ottawa?

_____

_____

9. Describe how the features of Ottawa differ from the town or city where you live.

_____

_____

_____

_____

Scale and Distance

A **map scale** compares distance on a map with distance in the real world. We use a map scale to find the distance between two places. A map scale shows distance in both **miles** (MI) and **kilometers** (KM). It looks like this:

```
0        220       440 MI
|---------|---------|
0        350       700 KM
```

► What do the letters MI and KM stand for?

► Which distance is longer, 400 miles or 400 kilometers?

Look at the map of the United States on page 23. Suppose you want to find the distance between Los Angeles and New York City. You will need a ruler, a pencil, and a piece of paper.

Here is how you use the map scale.

Step 1 Using your ruler, measure the distance between Los Angeles and New York City. On this map, Los Angeles and New York are 5½ inches apart.

Step 2 Look at the map scale in the lower right-hand corner. You can see that 1 inch equals 440 miles. Remember, there are 5½ inches between Los Angeles and New York City. Use multiplication to find the distance in miles or kilometers.

$$\begin{array}{r} \text{number of miles per inch} \quad 4\,4\,0 \\ \times \text{ number of inches} \quad \underline{\times \quad 5.5} \\ = \text{distance in miles} \quad \quad 2\,4\,2\,0 \end{array}$$

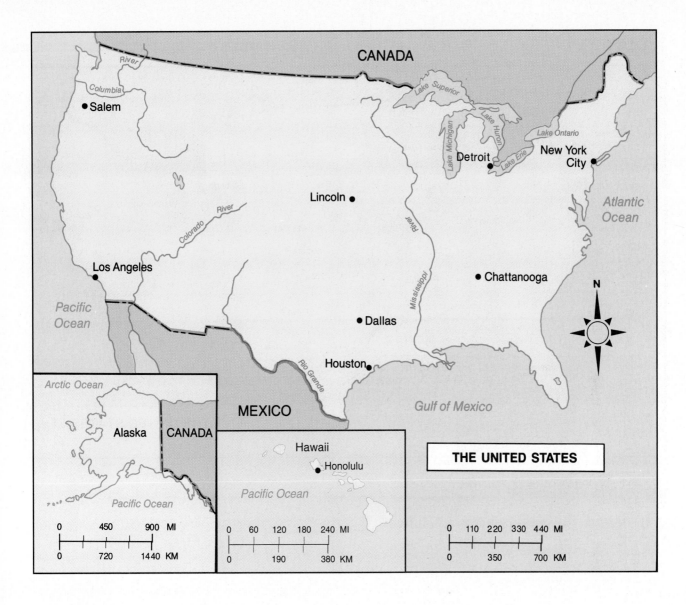

Look at the map of the United States above. Find the two smaller maps in the left-hand corner. One shows Alaska and the other shows Hawaii. Alaska and Hawaii are far from the other forty-eight states. This map isn't big enough to show where Alaska and Hawaii really are. So they are shown in inset maps.

An **inset map** is a small map within a larger map. An inset map may have its own scale. Map scales change depending on how much area is shown. Compare the map scales on the inset maps with the large map.

► One inch equals how many miles on the map of Hawaii?

► One inch equals how many miles on the map of Alaska?

► What can you tell about the sizes of Alaska and Hawaii?

► To figure the distance between Dallas and Houston, which map scale do you use?

► What is the distance between Dallas and Houston?

► Can you figure the distance between Honolulu and Los Angeles using these maps? Why or why not?

Figuring Distance in the United States

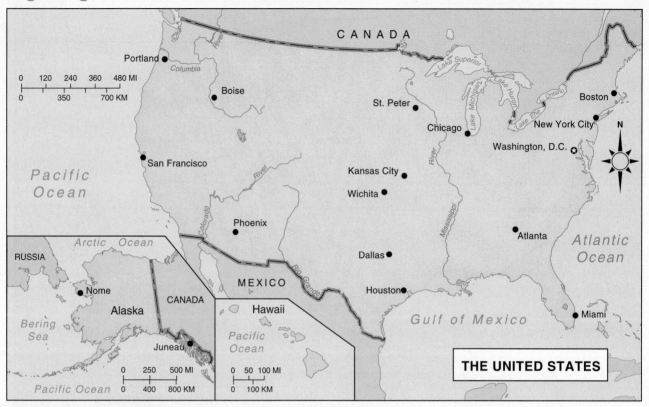

MAP ATTACK!

- **Read the title.** This map shows _____.
- **Read the map scale.** On the large map, one inch stands for

  _____ miles.

Use your ruler to figure these distances.

1. What two states are shown in the inset maps above? _____

   and _____

2. From Phoenix to Kansas City is about _____ miles.

3. From New York City to Washington, D.C. is about _____ miles.

4. From Kansas City to Boston is about _____ miles.

5. From Nome to Juneau is about _____ miles.

6. Is it farther from San Francisco to Houston or from Portland to Chicago?

   _____

Figuring Distance in the Great Lakes States

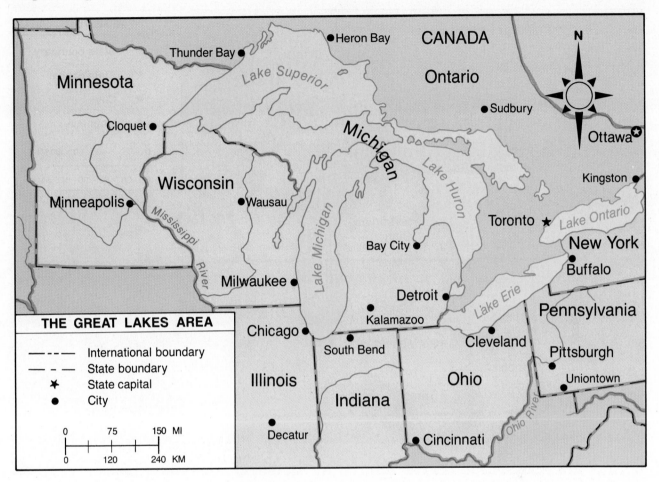

Use your ruler to figure these distances.

1. From Chicago to Decatur is about _____ miles.

2. From Wausau to Milwaukee is about _____ miles.

3. From Thunder Bay to Minneapolis is about _____ miles.

4. From Toronto to Buffalo is about _____ miles.

5. From Cleveland to Heron Bay is about _____ miles.

6. From Milwaukee to Ottawa is about _____ miles.

7. From Sudbury to Detroit is about _____ miles.

8. From Ottawa to Cincinnati is about _____ miles.
9. Is it farther from Chicago to Sudbury or from Heron Bay to Cleveland?

_____

10. Is it farther from Ottawa to Kingston or from Milwaukee to Chicago?

_____

Figuring Distance on a State Map

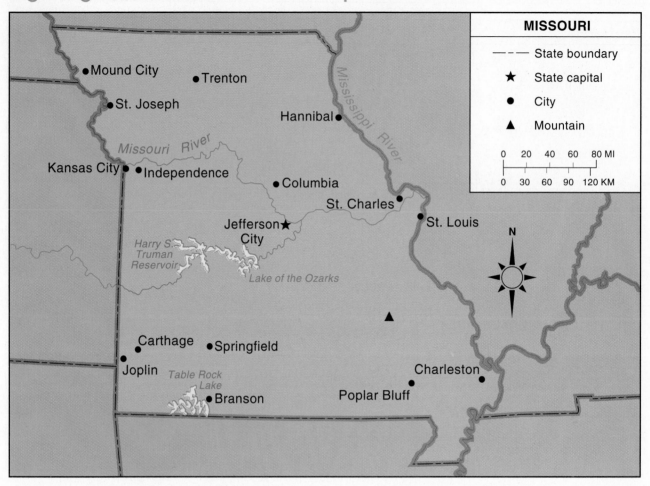

Imagine you are going on a tour of Missouri. Use a ruler to draw lines as you figure these distances and directions.

1. Find the state capital on the map. Circle it.

   a. What direction will you go from the state capital to Springfield? _____

   b. From the state capital to Springfield is about _____ miles.

2. a. What direction will you go from Springfield to Carthage? _____

   b. From Springfield to Carthage is about _____ miles.

3. a. What direction will you go from Carthage to Poplar Bluff? _____

   b. From Carthage to Poplar Bluff is about _____ miles.

4. a. What direction will you go from Poplar Bluff to St. Louis? _____

   b. From Poplar Bluff to St. Louis is about _____ miles.

5. There is a mountain about 80 miles southwest of St. Louis and about 60 miles northwest of Poplar Bluff. Find it on the map. Label it Taum Sauk Mountain. You have reached the highest point in Missouri!

Skill Check

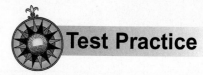

Vocabulary Check   map scale   miles   kilometers   inset map

Use each word or phrase to finish a sentence.

1. A map scale shows distance in _____ and

   _____.

2. A small map within a larger map is called an _____.

3. A _____ is used to compare distance on a map with distance on Earth.

Map Check

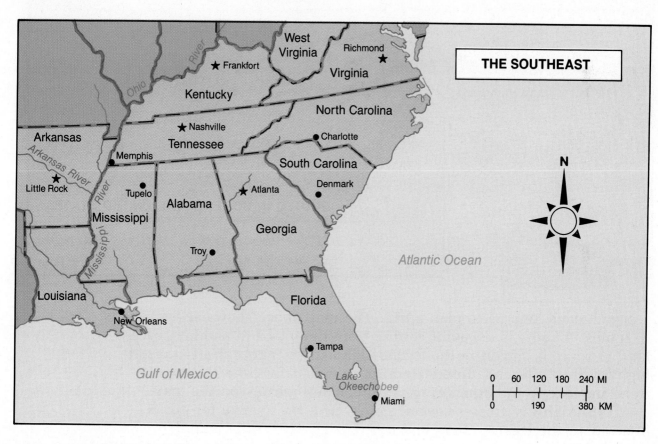

Use a ruler and the map scale to figure these distances.

1. From Atlanta to Richmond is about _____ miles.

2. From Memphis to Frankfort is about _____ miles.

3. From Nashville to Miami is about _____ miles.

4. Is it farther from Nashville to New Orleans or from Nashville to

   Richmond? _____

4 🌐 Route Maps

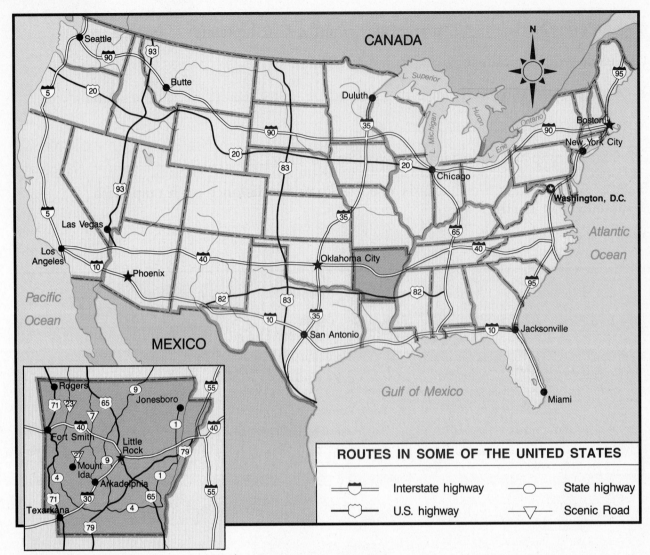

ROUTES IN SOME OF THE UNITED STATES

Interstate highway — State highway
U.S. highway — Scenic Road

Some maps help us to plan a trip. The map above shows several kinds of routes. A **route** is a way of getting from one place to another. Each kind of route is shown in the legend. Find the symbol for an interstate highway in the legend. **Interstate highways** usually cross the country from one side to the other. Find an interstate highway on the map.

A **U.S. highway** crosses several states. Find the symbol for a U.S. highway in the legend. Then find a U.S. highway on the map.

State highways connect cities and towns within one state. **Scenic roads** cross areas that offer a beautiful view. Find the symbols for state highway and scenic road. Look at the inset map of Arkansas. What kinds of routes do you see?

► Interstate 35 connects what northern city with what southern city?

► U.S. 93 connects Las Vegas with the boundary of what country?

► What state highway crosses southern Arkansas?

► Where are the scenic roads in Arkansas?

► What U.S. highway passes through Little Rock?

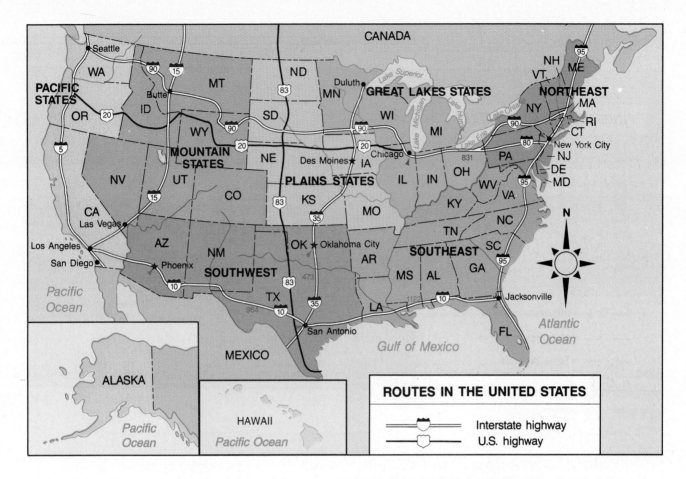

Look at the route map above. It shows interstate and U.S. highways crossing regions of the United States. A **region** is an area with many things in common. Find the Pacific States. Notice that all of the Pacific States touch the Pacific Ocean. What states are included in this region?

Three regions are named for intermediate directions. Find them. Name the states in the Southwest, the Southeast, and the Northeast.

Three regions are named for land or water forms. Find them. Name the states in the Mountain States, the Plains States, and the Great Lakes States.

Route maps often show the distance between cities. Find the small red triangle pointing to Chicago. That triangle is a **mileage marker**. The next mileage marker east of Chicago is in New York City. The distance from Chicago to New York City is 831 miles. Find the red number 831 near the route from Chicago to New York City.

► What lakes border the Great Lakes States?

► What regions does Interstate 10 cross?

► What regions does U.S. 83 cross?

► What interstate crosses the Mountain States from north to south?

► What U.S. highway crosses the Plains States from north to south?

► What highways would take you from Seattle to Las Vegas via (by way of) Butte?

► What is the distance from San Antonio to Jacksonville?

Reading a Route Map

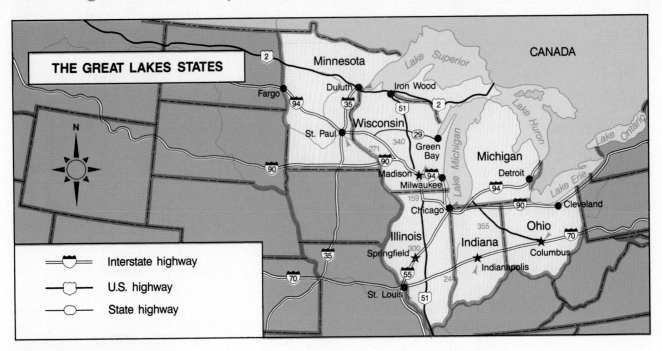

MAP ATTACK!

● **Read the title.** This map shows _____.

● **Read the legend.** The three types of highways shown are _____,

_____, and _____.

● **Read the compass rose.** Label the intermediate directions.

1. What states are included in this region? _____

_____

2. Which of the Great Lakes border this region?

_____

3. Trace the route from Green Bay to St. Paul. Use a green pencil or

marker. What highways would you take? _____

4. Trace the route from Green Bay to Duluth via Iron Wood. Use a red

pencil or marker. What highways would you take? _____

5. Is it farther from Chicago to St. Louis or from Chicago to Columbus?

_____

6. Where would you see this sign?

Duluth	340
St. Paul	271
Chicago	159

Reading a Route Map

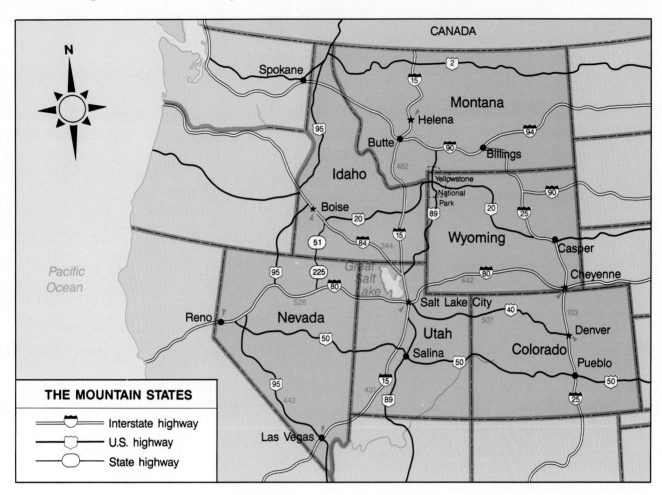

THE MOUNTAIN STATES

— Interstate highway
— U.S. highway
— State highway

1. What region is shown here? _____

2. What states are in this region? _____

_____

3. Trace the route from Helena to Salt Lake City in green.

   a. What highway takes you from Helena to Salt Lake City? _____

   b. How many miles is it from Helena to Salt Lake City? _____

   c. What states do you cross? _____

4. Trace the route from Helena to Cheyenne in orange. Be sure to go through Yellowstone National Park.

   What highways would you take? _____

5. What U.S. highway connects Interstate 84 with Interstate 80? _____

6. Where would you see this sign? _____
   (I stands for Interstate.)

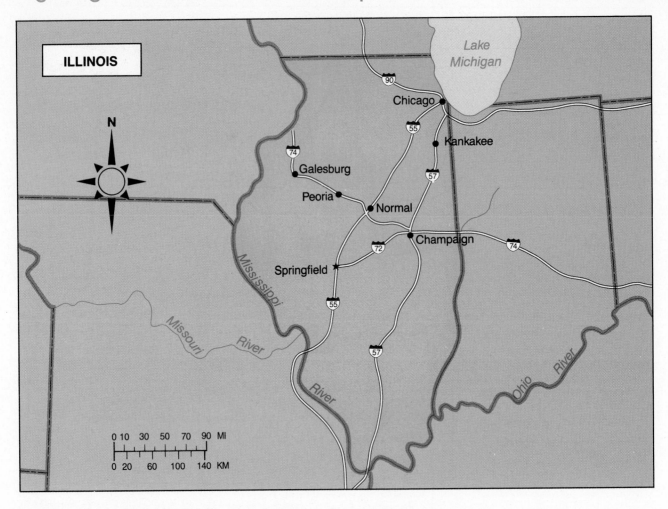

1. Circle the capital of Illinois on the map. Name it. _____
2. Chicago is the largest city in Illinois. Find it on the map and circle it.
3. From Chicago to Springfield is about _____ miles.
4. You want to find the shortest route from Chicago to Springfield. Would you drive Interstate 57 and Interstate 72 or Interstate 55 through

   Normal? _____

   What direction would you be traveling? _____

5. From Kankakee to Champaign is about _____ miles.

   What direction is Champaign from Kankakee? _____

6. From Springfield to Champaign is about _____ miles.

   What direction is Champaign from Springfield? _____

7. If you drove 40 miles an hour from Springfield to Champaign, how many

   hours would it take? _____

Skill Check

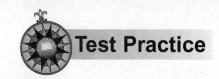

Vocabulary Check

route	interstate highway	U.S. highway
state highway	scenic road	region
mileage marker		

1. An _____ crosses the entire country.

2. A _____ crosses several states.

3. To figure distances on route maps, use the _____.

4. A _____ crosses one state.

5. An area with many things in common is a _____.

Map Check

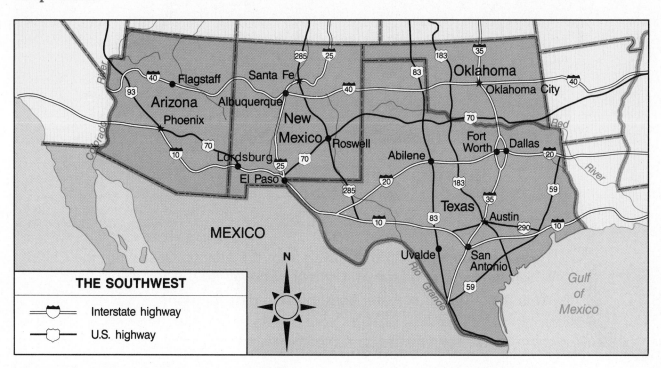

THE SOUTHWEST

Interstate highway

U.S. highway

1. What interstate highway splits to go through Dallas and Fort Worth? ____

2. What route goes <u>through</u> the capital of Arizona? _____

3. What route goes along part of the Red River? _____

4. What route goes through both the capital of Oklahoma and the capital

   of Texas? _____

5. What interstate highways would you take from Flagstaff to Abilene via

   Albuquerque and El Paso? _____

Geography Themes Up Close

Movement describes how people, goods, information, and ideas move from place to place. Movement shows people interacting. It demonstrates **interdependence**, or how people depend on one another, to meet their needs and wants. The St. Lawrence Seaway is a waterway that connects the Atlantic Ocean with the Great Lakes. This waterway lies in Canada and in the United States.

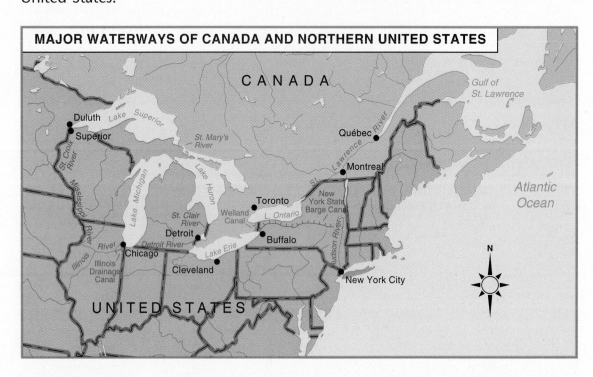

MAJOR WATERWAYS OF CANADA AND NORTHERN UNITED STATES

1. Trace the route of a ship that travels from the Atlantic Ocean into the Gulf of St. Lawrence, through the St. Lawrence Seaway, to the Mississippi River.

2. What major bodies of water does this ship pass through?

_____

_____

_____

3. What cities would the ship pass on its way to Chicago?

_____

4. What major bodies of water would a ship pass through, traveling from Duluth to New York City?

_____

_____

5. How do these waterways show interdependence and make the movement of people and goods easier between people in the United States and Canada?

_____

_____

_____

Charts show facts in columns and rows. The chart below shows facts about using communication tools.

Use of Communication Tools in the United States

Number of hours per person per year			
	1995	2000	2005 (est.)
Television	1,575	1,633	1,679
Radio	1,091	961	998
Newspapers	165	151	144
Books	99	90	84
Magazines	84	107	100
Internet	7	124	194

6. According to the chart, which communication tool is most used by people in

the United States? _____

7. Which communication tool is used the least in the United States? Why do you think this is so?

_____

_____

_____

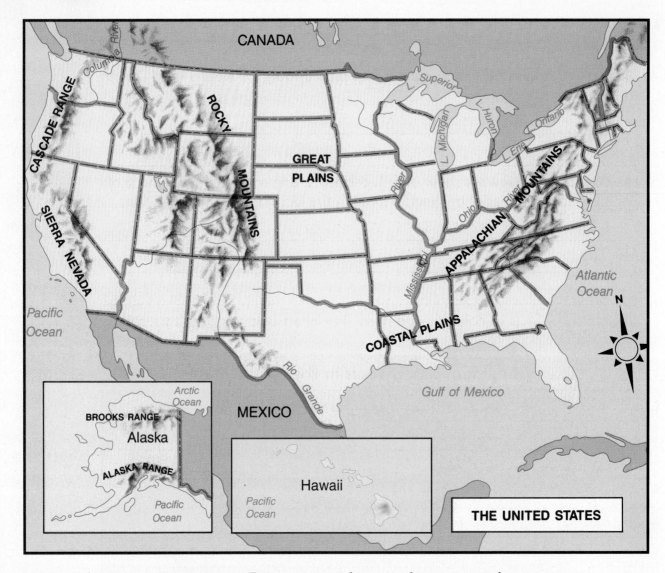

THE UNITED STATES

Maps have many purposes. Route maps show us how to get from one place to another. **Relief maps** show different landforms on Earth. Look at the relief map above. It shows the United States. You can see mountain ranges, plains, lakes, and rivers.

A **mountain range** is a group or chain of mountains. Find the Rocky Mountains on the map. A **plain** is a large area of level, treeless land. Now find the Great Plains. Which is darker, the mountains or the plains?

Relief maps help us picture how the land looks. The dark shading on relief maps stands for mountains. Higher mountains appear the darkest. Since plains are very flat, we do not see any shading.

► Locate your own state. Is your state mostly mountains or plains?

► Name the mountain ranges and plains shown on the map.

► What is the highest mountain range on the map? How do you know?

► Are there more mountains in the eastern or in the western United States?

► Locate the inset map of Alaska. Are there more mountains or plains?

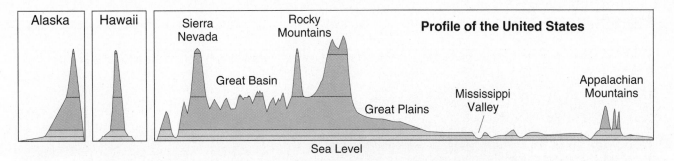

Profile of the United States

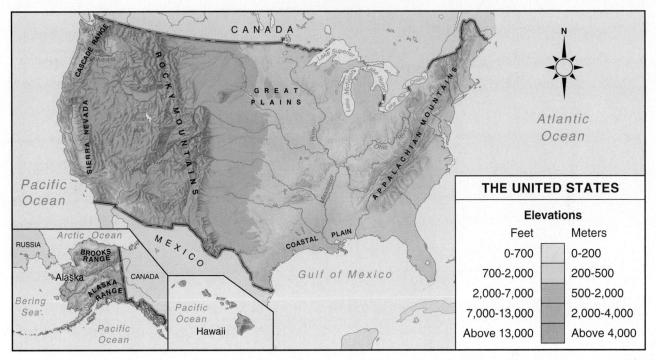

THE UNITED STATES		
Elevations		
Feet		Meters
0-700		0-200
700-2,000		200-500
2,000-7,000		500-2,000
7,000-13,000		2,000-4,000
Above 13,000		Above 4,000

Sea level is the level of the ocean surface. Land that is even with the ocean is at sea level. Land that is higher than the ocean is above sea level. **Elevation** means the height of the land above sea level. Look at the diagram. It shows a side-view of the mountains, valleys, and plains of the United States. Each color in the legend and diagram stands for a different elevation. Elevation is measured in feet or meters.

A **physical map** combines elevation and relief. The physical maps above show the United States. The colors in the legend tell you the elevation of the land. This makes it easy to understand what the United States really looks like. Physical maps may also show cities, boundaries, mountain peaks, and rivers.

► On the map above, what color shows the elevation of the highest mountain peaks?

► What color is used to show the elevation of the Great Plains?

► Locate the area on the map where you live.
What is the elevation of the area where you live?

► Find the Rocky Mountains in the diagram. What colors are used to show their elevation? Find the Rocky Mountains on the map. What colors are used to show their elevation?

Reading a Physical Map

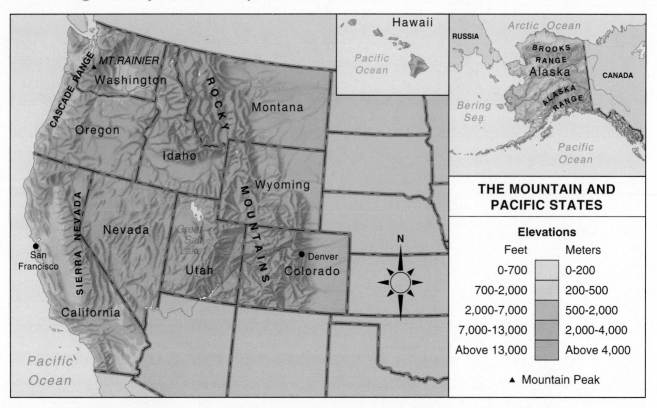

MAP ATTACK!

- **Read the title.** This map shows _____.

- **Read the legend.** What color is land above 13,000 feet? _____
- **Read the compass rose.** Circle the intermediate direction arrows.

1. Which color in the legend stands for the lowest elevation? _____

Complete each sentence below.

2. Find the Great Salt Lake in Utah. The elevation of this area is between

   2,000 and 7,000 feet or between _____ and _____ meters.

3. Find Denver, Colorado. The elevation of this city is between _____

   and _____ feet or between _____ and _____ meters.

4. Find San Francisco, California. The elevation of this city is

   between _____ and _____ feet or between _____ and

   _____ meters.

5. Find the symbol for mountain peak in the legend. What is the name of a

   mountain peak in the state of Washington? _____

Reading a Physical Map

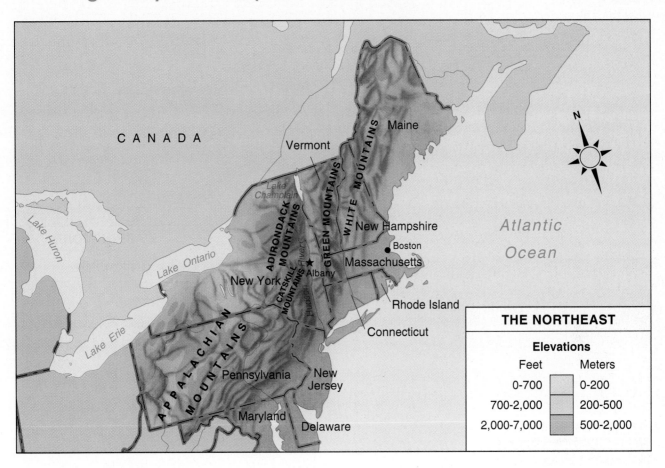

1. Look at the land along the coast of the Atlantic Ocean. Is this land

   mountainous or flat?_____

2. Which state has only low elevation and is all the same color?

   _____

3. Which are higher, the Catskill Mountains or the White Mountains?

   _____

4. What lake lies near the northwestern edge of the Green Mountains?

   _____

5. Trace the Hudson River. The Hudson River flows into what body of

   water?_____

6. The elevation of Boston is between _____ and _____ feet or

   between _____ and _____ meters.

7. Draw a conclusion. Would it be easy to hike from the White Mountains

   to Albany? Why or why not?_____

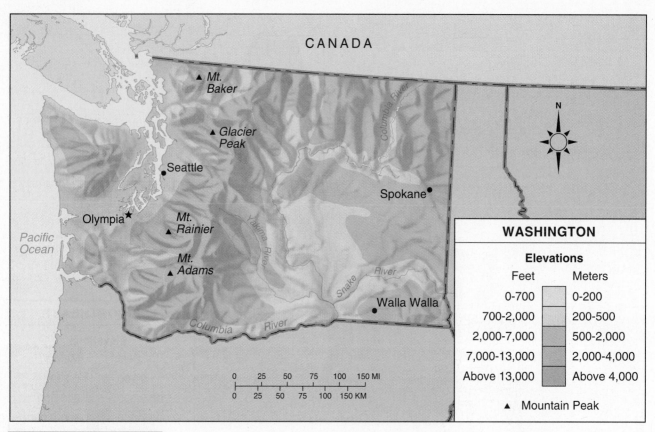

MAP ATTACK!

Follow the steps on page 38 to begin reading this map.

1. What is the state capital of Washington?_____

2. The elevation of the state capital is between _____ and _____ feet.

3. What direction is Seattle from the state capital? _____

4. How many miles is it from the state capital to Seattle? Use a ruler and the map scale. The distance is about _____ miles.

5. From Seattle, which direction would you travel to reach an international border? _____

6. From Seattle, which direction would you travel to reach a boundary formed by a river? _____

7. Which is higher, Seattle or Spokane? _____

8. Draw a conclusion. Draw a line from Walla Walla to Seattle. What problems would you face if you built a highway from Walla Walla to Seattle? _____

Skill Check

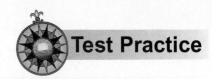

Vocabulary Check   relief map   plain   mountain range
                                         physical map   elevation

1. The height of the land in feet or meters is called _____.

2. A _____ is a group of mountains.

3. A _____ shows the landforms on Earth.

4. A _____ is a large area of flat land.

5. A map that shows changes in elevation is called a _____.

Map Check

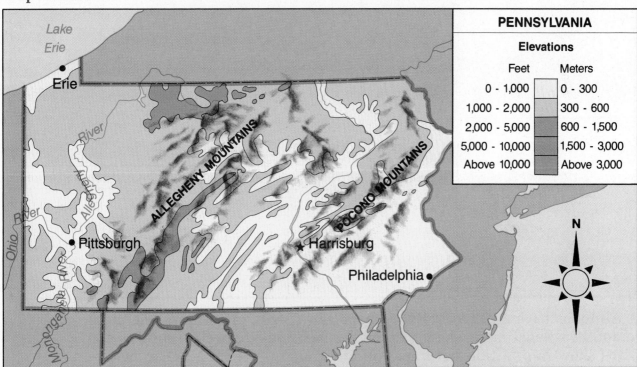

1. Which mountains are higher, the Allegheny Mountains or the Pocono

   Mountains? _____
2. What three rivers meet in Pittsburgh?

   _____

3. Is Erie at a higher or lower elevation than Philadelphia? _____

4. What is the state capital of Pennsylvania? _____

5. The elevation of the state capital is between _____ and _____

   feet or between _____ and _____ meters.

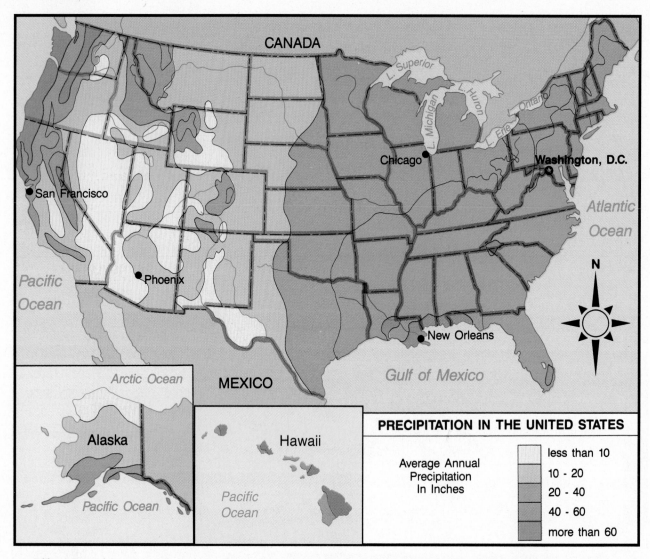

PRECIPITATION IN THE UNITED STATES

Average Annual Precipitation In Inches

	less than 10
	10 - 20
	20 - 40
	40 - 60
	more than 60

All maps have a purpose. Route maps show ways to get from one place to another. Relief maps show us how the land looks. **Special purpose** maps show information not found on other maps. The information may be about the climate, the people, the resources, or the history of an area. You need to read each map's title and legend carefully.

Use the map reading skills you've learned to read a special purpose map. Read the title carefully. The title tells you what the map shows. This map shows precipitation in the United States. Precipitation is rain and snow.

Read the legend carefully. The legend tells you what the symbols mean. On this map, colors are used as symbols. Remember that a **symbol** is something that stands for something else. Here each color stands for a different amount of precipitation.

► What color stands for 20-40 inches of precipitation per year?
What areas on the map get 20-40 inches of precipitation per year?

► Does more precipitation fall along the coastlines or inland?

► Which areas of the United States get the most precipitation?

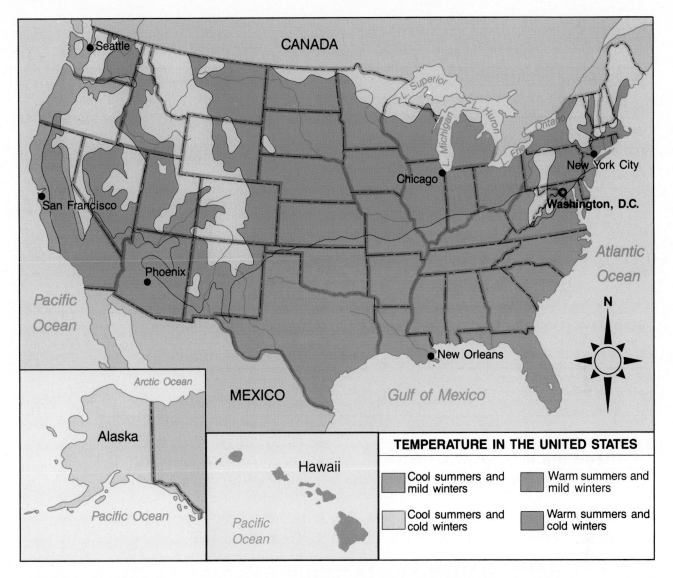

TEMPERATURE IN THE UNITED STATES

Cool summers and mild winters	Warm summers and mild winters
Cool summers and cold winters	Warm summers and cold winters

There are many types of special purpose maps. A **resource map** uses symbols for things in nature that people can use. In the legend you may find symbols for things like gold, oil, or coal. These symbols will appear on the map in the area where the resource is found.

Population maps show the number of people living in an area. The population of an area may be shown by using colors, dots of different sizes, or both.

Above is a **temperature map**. The legend shows summer and winter temperatures in the United States. It tells you that green areas have warm summers and cold winters. What color shows warm summers and mild winters?

► What kind of temperatures does New York City have?

► Look at the inset maps. What kind of temperatures do Alaska and Hawaii have?

► What kind of temperatures does Seattle have?

► Locate your state on the map on page 42 and the map above. Describe the climate where you live. What kind of temperatures and how much precipitation does your state have?

Reading a Historical Map

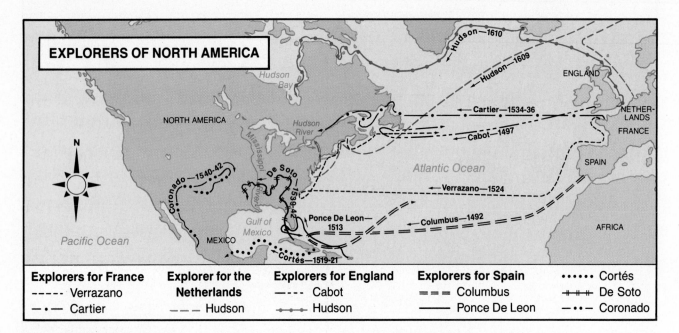

EXPLORERS OF NORTH AMERICA

Hudson—1610
Hudson—1609
ENGLAND
Hudson Bay
NORTH AMERICA
Hudson River
Cartier—1534-36
NETHER-LANDS
Cabot—1497
FRANCE
SPAIN
Atlantic Ocean
N
Coronado—1540-42
De Soto 1539-42
Mississippi River
Verrazano—1524
Ponce De Leon—1513
Columbus—1492
AFRICA
Pacific Ocean
Gulf of Mexico
MEXICO
Cortés—1519-21

Explorers for France	Explorer for the Netherlands	Explorers for England	Explorers for Spain	
----- Verrazano	——— Hudson	—--- Cabot	=== Columbus	•••••• Cortés
—•— Cartier		•—•—• Hudson	——— Ponce De Leon	++++ De Soto
				—••— Coronado

MAP ATTACK!

- **Read the title.** This map shows _____.
- **Read the legend.** Check (✔) each symbol as you read its meaning.
- **Read the compass rose.** Label the intermediate direction arrows.

1. Find Columbus in the legend. What color shows his voyage? _____

2. In what country did Columbus start? _____

3. Which explorer made two trips to the New World? _____

   a. Where did he begin his first voyage? _____

   b. In what years were his voyages? _____
   c. What is a body of water named after this explorer?

   _____

4. Trace DeSoto's route in red.

   What river did he cross? _____
5. Trace Coronado's route in blue.

   In what country did he start? _____

6. DeSoto and Coronado were explorers for what country? _____
7. Draw a conclusion. Did most of the explorers for Spain travel to the

   northern or southern regions of North America? _____

Reading a Population Map

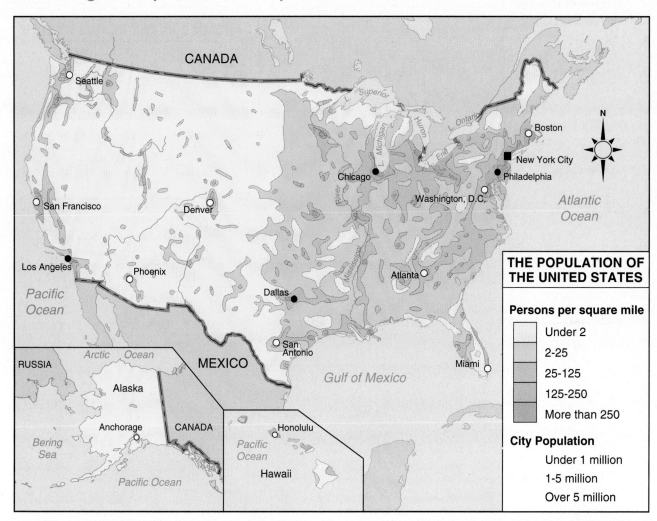

THE POPULATION OF THE UNITED STATES

Persons per square mile

- Under 2
- 2-25
- 25-125
- 125-250
- More than 250

City Population

- Under 1 million
- 1-5 million
- Over 5 million

1. The purpose of this map is to show

_____.

2. What color shows less than 2 people per square mile? _____

3. Do you find more of this color in the eastern or in the western United

   States? _____

4. What color shows more than 500 people per square mile? _____

5. Add these symbols to the legend.   ○ City of under 1 million

   ● 1–5 million

   ■ Over 5 million

6. Name three cities that have 1 to 5 million people _____

   _____ and _____

7. What city has the largest population? _____

Reading a Land Use Map

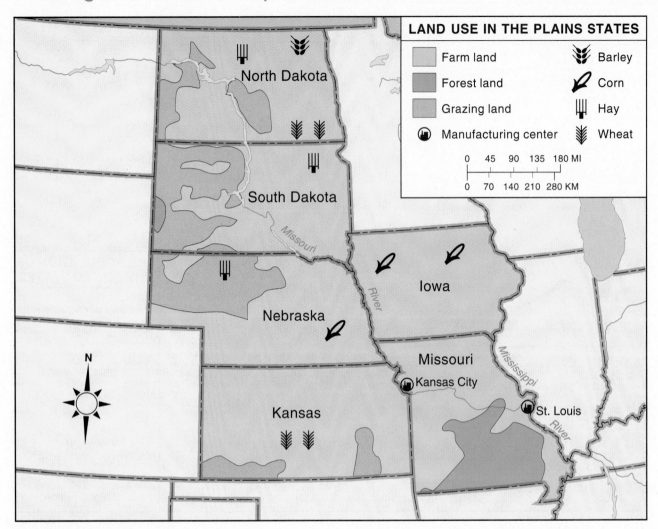

LAND USE IN THE PLAINS STATES

- Farm land
- Forest land
- Grazing land
- Manufacturing center
- Barley
- Corn
- Hay
- Wheat

0 45 90 135 180 MI

0 70 140 210 280 KM

MAP ATTACK!

Follow the steps on page 44 to begin reading this map.

1. The purpose of this map is to show _____.

2. What is the most common use of land in these states? _____

3. In which state is barley grown? _____

4. In which states is corn grown? _____

5. What is the most common use of land in western South Dakota?

   _____

6. In what part of Kansas is there grazing land? _____

7. There are two manufacturing centers in this region. Circle them.

   a. What are they? _____

   b. About how far apart are they? _____

Skill Check

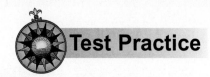

Vocabulary Check   **special purpose map   temperature map   symbol**
                           resource map   population map

Write the word that makes each sentence true.

1. A map showing the number of people in an area is a _____.

2. A map showing special information is a _____.

3. A _____ shows things found in nature that people can use.

Map Check

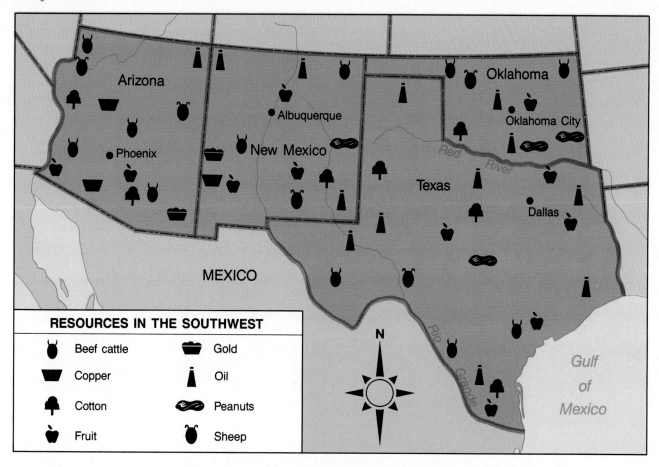

1. Gold is found in which states? _____

2. Is there more oil in Arizona or in Texas? _____

3. Cotton can be found in every state on this map. Name two other

   resources that can be found in all four states. _____

4. Which state does not grow peanuts? _____

5. Copper is found in which two states? _____

Geography Themes Up Close

Human/Environment Interaction shows how the environment and people affect one another. Sometimes people create problems. An example is pollution. One kind of pollution is **acid rain**—pollution that mixes with water vapor and falls to the ground in the form of rain or snow. This pollution comes from factories, power plants, and cars and trucks that burn coal, oil, and gas. Acid rain kills fish and destroys forests. It pollutes drinking water and soil and damages buildings. The map below shows recent acid rain levels in the United States and Canada.

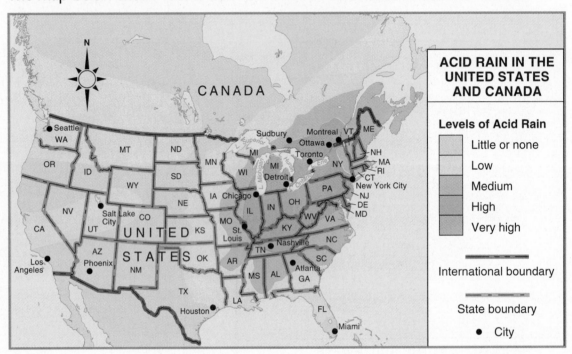

1. According to the map, where are the highest levels of acid rain found?

_____

_____

_____

2. Describe acid rain levels in western Canada and the western United States.

_____

3. Based on the map, where do you think most manufacturing centers are located in the United States and Canada? Explain your answer.

_____

_____

_____

Human/Environment Interaction includes how people depend on the environment. The map shown here demonstrates how people in Mexico use the land and its resources to meet their needs and wants.

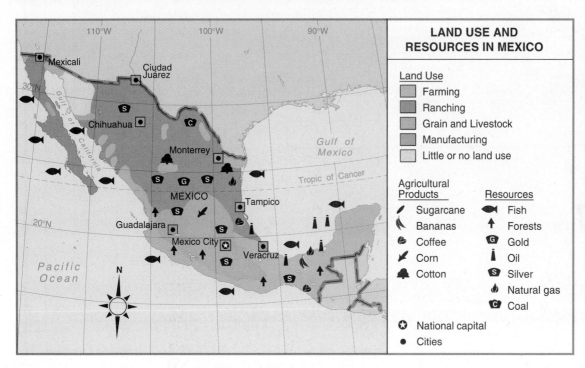

4. According to the map, where is fishing an important activity?

_____

5. Where is manufacturing an important activity?

_____

6. Where is most of the farming done in Mexico?

_____

7. Based on the map key and map, where would you expect Mexico's population to be the smallest?

_____

8. Along which of these coasts would be a better location for oil refineries: Pacific Ocean, Gulf of Mexico, or Gulf of California? Why?

_____

_____

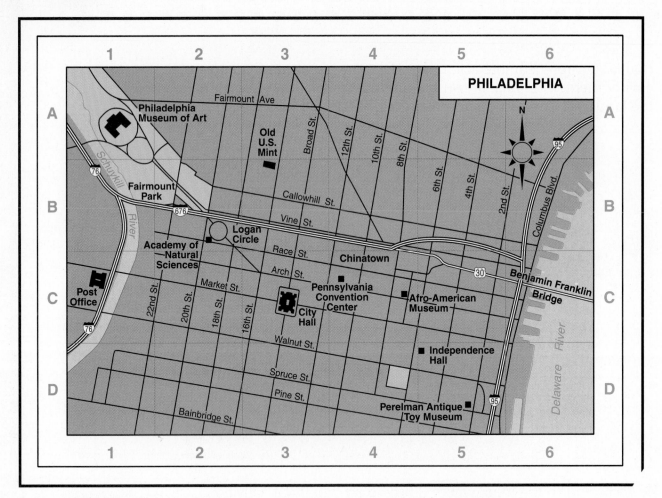

A **grid** is a pattern of lines drawn on a map to help people locate places. These lines form squares. Do you see the squares on the map above?

Now find the letters at each side of the map. The letters label the rows of squares. Numbers at the top and bottom label the columns of squares.

Locate City Hall on the map above. It is in square C-3. Find the letter C on the left side of the map. Slide your finger across row C until you reach column 3. You are now in square C-3. Put your finger on City Hall.

► Now move your finger one square to the east.
  This is square C-4. Name two points of interest in C-4.

► Find the Perelman Antique Toy Museum. It is in square D-5.
  Name another historic site in this square that you could visit.

► The Philadelphia Museum of Art is in square A-1.
  This museum is in what park?
  Put your finger on the museum. Slide it southeast through the park.
  The park ends near Logan Circle. In what grid square is Logan Circle?

► Locate the Benjamin Franklin Bridge in square C-6.
  What river does it cross?
  Can you name the other grid squares that this river flows through?

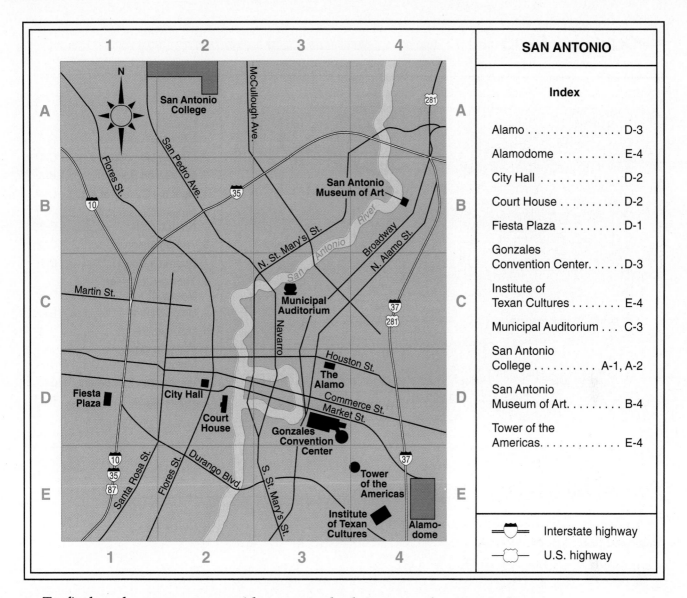

To find a place on a map grid, you can look it up in the map index. A **map index** is an alphabetical list of all the places shown on the map. A map index lists each place with the letter and number of its grid square.

Look at the map above. It shows places of interest in San Antonio, Texas. To find places on the map, you use the map index. Imagine you want to visit the Alamo. Look up "Alamo" in the map index. It directs you to square D-3. Locate square D-3 on the grid. Do you see the Alamo?

► Use the map index to find City Hall. In what grid square is it located? Find City Hall on the map. Name another point of interest in this square.

► Look up the San Antonio Museum of Art in the map index. In what grid square is it located? What direction is the San Antonio Museum of Art from City Hall?

► Find San Antonio College by using the map index. In what grid squares is it located?

► Locate the Institute of Texan Cultures using the map index. In what grid square is it located? What other points of interest are located in this same square?

Reading a Map Grid

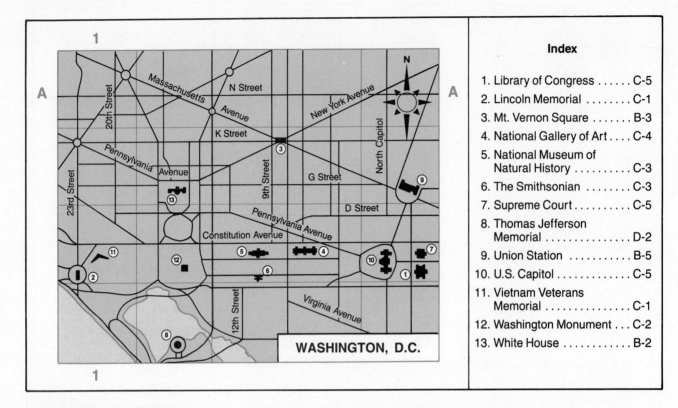

Index

1. Library of Congress C-5
2. Lincoln Memorial C-1
3. Mt. Vernon Square B-3
4. National Gallery of Art C-4
5. National Museum of
   Natural History C-3
6. The Smithsonian C-3
7. Supreme Court C-5
8. Thomas Jefferson
   Memorial D-2
9. Union Station B-5
10. U.S. Capitol C-5
11. Vietnam Veterans
    Memorial C-1
12. Washington Monument ... C-2
13. White House B-2

WASHINGTON, D.C.

MAP ATTACK!

● **Read the title.** This map shows _____ .
● **Read the compass rose.** Circle the north arrow. Label the
  intermediate directions.
● **Read the grid.** Add the missing letters and numbers.

Use the index and map to answer these questions.

1. In what square is the White House located? _____
   Circle it on the map.

2. In what square is the Washington Monument? _____
   Circle it on the map.
   What famous memorial is south of the Washington Monument?

   _____

   What memorial is to the northwest? _____

3. In what square is the U.S. Capitol located? _____

   What two points of interest are to the east? _____

   _____

Reading a Map Grid

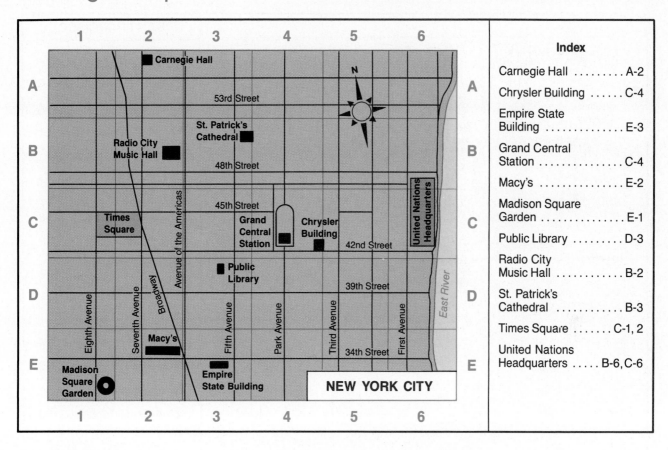

1. In what squares is the United Nations Headquarters located? _____
   What avenue goes along the west side of the United Nations

   Headquarters? _____

2. In what grid squares is Times Square located? _____
   Draw a line along 42nd Street from the United Nations Headquarters
   to Times Square.

   Name one building you pass. _____

3. In what grid square is Radio City Music Hall located? _____
   Trace your route from Times Square to Radio City Music Hall.
   What avenue is just east of Radio City Music Hall?

   _____

4. In what grid square is the Empire State Building? _____
   Trace your route from Radio City Music Hall east to Fifth Avenue.
   Trace your route to the Empire State Building.
   What street is just north of the Empire State Building?

   _____

Reading a Map Grid

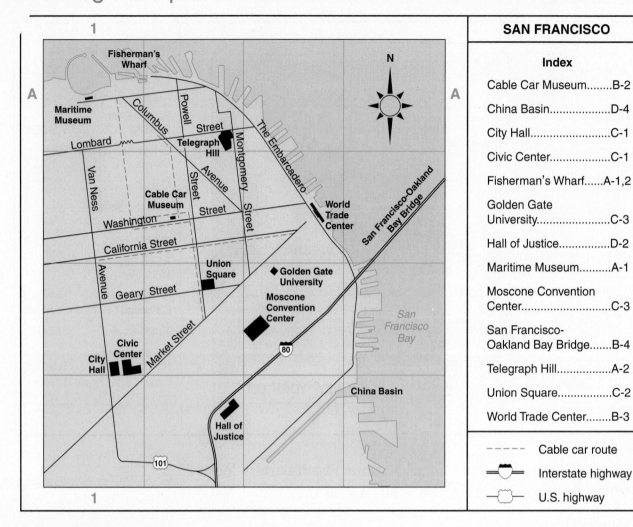

- - - - - Cable car route

Interstate highway

U.S. highway

MAP ATTACK!

Follow the steps on page 52 to begin reading this map.

1. In what grid square do you find the Maritime Museum? _____
   Circle it on the map.

2. In what grid square is the Cable Car Museum located? _____
   Circle it on the map.

3. What direction is the Maritime Museum from the Cable Car Museum?

   _____

4. Trace the cable car route from the Cable Car Museum to Union Square.

   Is Union Square east or west of the cable car route? _____

5. What interstate highway is in San Francisco? _____

6. What U.S. highway is in San Francisco? _____

Skill Check

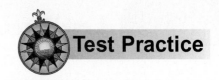

Vocabulary Check   **grid**   **map index**

1. A pattern of lines drawn on a map is called a _____.

2. A _____ is an alphabetized list of all the places shown on a map.

Map Check

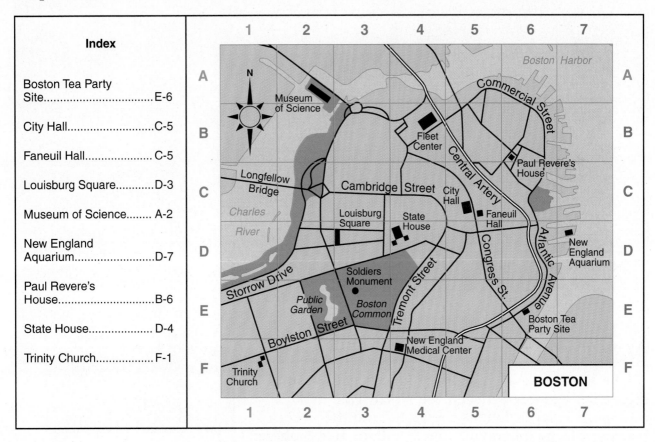

Index	
Boston Tea Party Site	E-6
City Hall	C-5
Faneuil Hall	C-5
Louisburg Square	D-3
Museum of Science	A-2
New England Aquarium	D-7
Paul Revere's House	B-6
State House	D-4
Trinity Church	F-1

1. Complete the grid by adding the missing letters and numbers.

2. In what grid square do you find City Hall? _____
   Circle it.

3. In what grid square do you find Paul Revere's House? _____

   What direction is Paul Revere's House from City Hall? _____

4. In what grid square is the New England Aquarium located? _____

   What direction is the Aquarium from Paul Revere's House? _____

5. In what grid square is the Boston Tea Party Site located? _____

   What direction is it from City Hall? _____

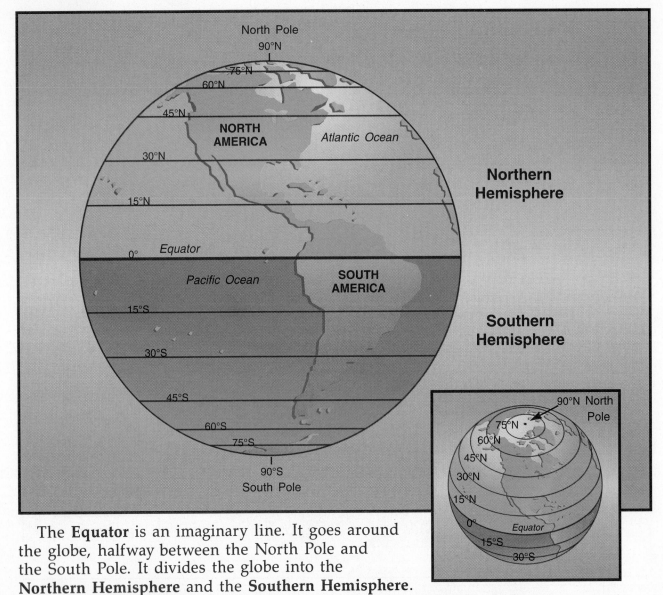

The **Equator** is an imaginary line. It goes around the globe, halfway between the North Pole and the South Pole. It divides the globe into the **Northern Hemisphere** and the **Southern Hemisphere**. Remember that the globe is a sphere. A **hemisphere** is half of a sphere.

The Equator is the most important line of **latitude**. The other lines of latitude measure distance on a globe north or south of the Equator. We use lines of latitude to locate places on the globe.

► Find the Equator on the large globe above.
  It is marked 0°. The symbol ° stands for **degrees**.

► Find the 45°N line of latitude. What continent does it cross?

► Find the 45°S line of latitude. What continent does it cross?

Lines of latitude are also called **parallels**. Lines of latitude never touch.

► Look at the small globe above.
  Find the 75°N parallel.
  Does it touch any other parallel?
  What continents does it cross?

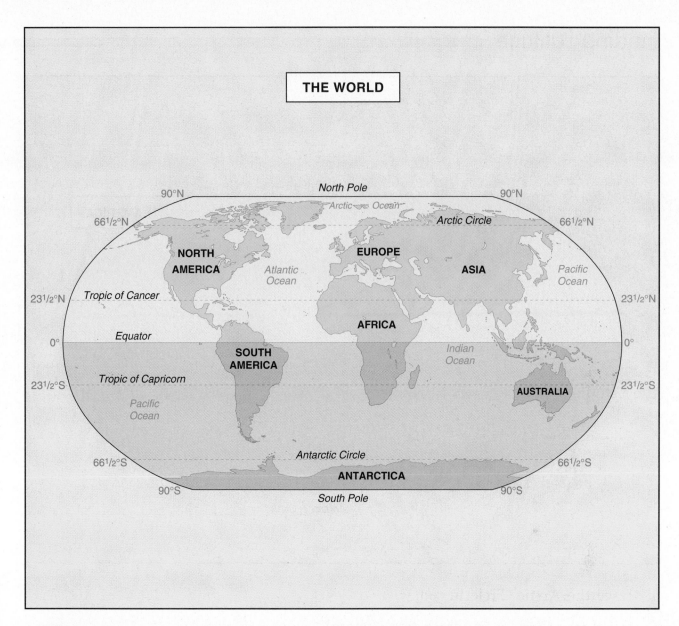

THE WORLD

There are some other important parallels. You know that 0° latitude is called the Equator. Other lines of latitude also have names. Find the line south of the Equator marked 23½°S. That line is called the **Tropic of Capricorn**.

Find the line north of the Equator marked 23½°N. That line is called the **Tropic of Cancer**.

Two other important lines of latitude are the **Arctic Circle** and the **Antarctic Circle**. The Arctic Circle is 66½°N of the Equator. Find the Arctic Circle on the map above. The Antarctic Circle is 66½°S of the Equator. Find the Antarctic Circle on the map above.

► The Tropic of Cancer goes through which continents?

► The Tropic of Capricorn goes through which oceans?

► The Arctic Circle goes through which continents?

► The Antarctic Circle goes around which continent?

► Which important parallel do you live nearest?

Finding Latitude

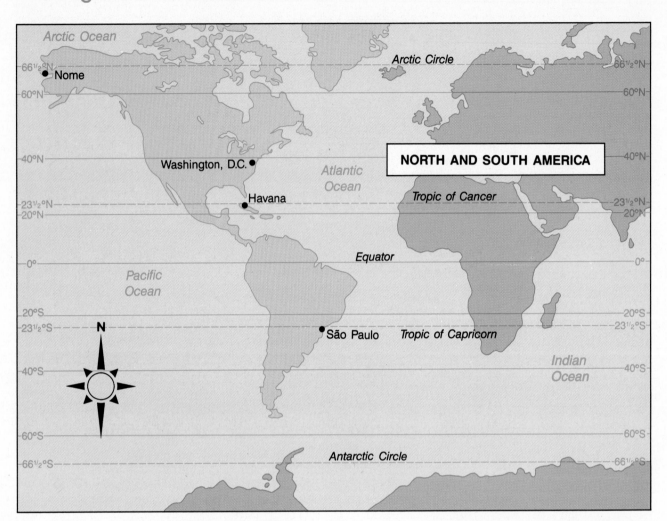

1. Trace the Arctic Circle in red.

   The Arctic Circle is in which hemisphere? _____

   What city lies near the Arctic Circle? _____
2. Trace the Antarctic Circle in blue.

   The Antarctic Circle is in which hemisphere? _____

   What oceans does the Antarctic Circle touch? _____
3. Trace the Tropic of Cancer in orange.

   The Tropic of Cancer is in which hemisphere? _____

   What city lies near the Tropic of Cancer? _____
4. Trace the Tropic of Capricorn in green. The Tropic of Capricorn

   is in which hemisphere? _____

   What city lies near the Tropic of Capricorn? _____

Finding Latitude

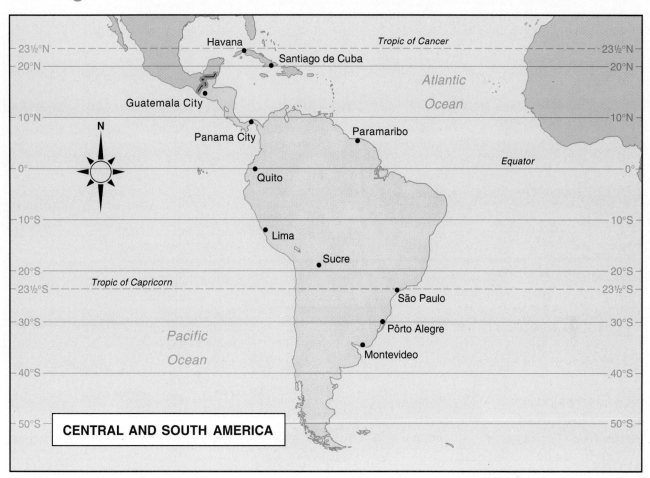

CENTRAL AND SOUTH AMERICA

1. What city lies on the Equator? _____

2. What city lies near the Tropic of Cancer? _____

3. What city lies near the Tropic of Capricorn? _____

4. What city lies near 20°N? _____

5. What city lies near 10°N? _____

6. What city lies near 20°S? _____

7. What city lies at 30°S? _____

8. Guatemala City lies between 20°N and 10°N.

    Estimate its latitude. _____

9. Paramaribo lies between 10°N and the Equator.

    Estimate its latitude. _____

10. Montevideo lies between 30°S and 40°S.

    Estimate its latitude. _____

Finding Latitude

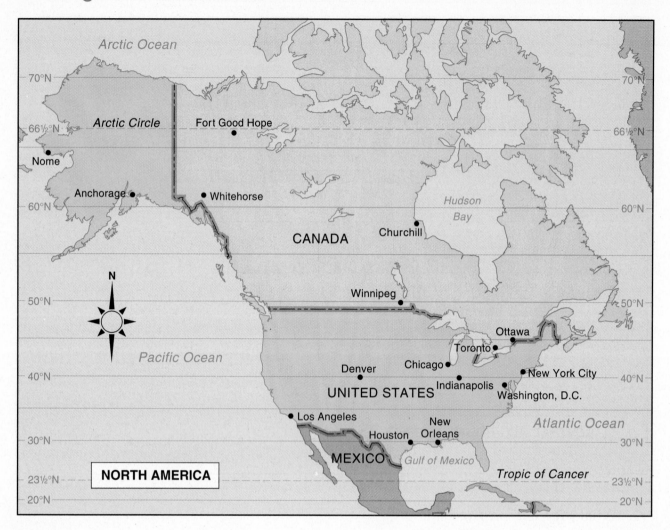

1. What two cities lie at 30°N? _____

2. What two cities lie at 40°N? _____

3. What city lies at 50°N? _____

4. What is another name for 66½°N latitude? _____

5. What city lies near the Arctic Circle?_____

6. Find Ottawa. It lies between 40°N and 50°N.

   Estimate its latitude. _____

7. Find Los Angeles. It lies between 30°N and 40°N.

   Estimate its latitude. _____

8. What border runs along the 49°N line of latitude?

   _____

9. Is Canada north or south of the Tropic of Cancer? _____

Skill Check

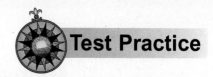
Vocabulary Check

Equator	latitude	parallcl
Tropic of Capricorn	Tropic of Cancer	degrees
Arctic Circle	Antarctic Circle	
Northern Hemisphere	Southern Hemisphere	

1. Another name for a line of latitude is a _____.

2. Latitude is measured in _____.

Map Check

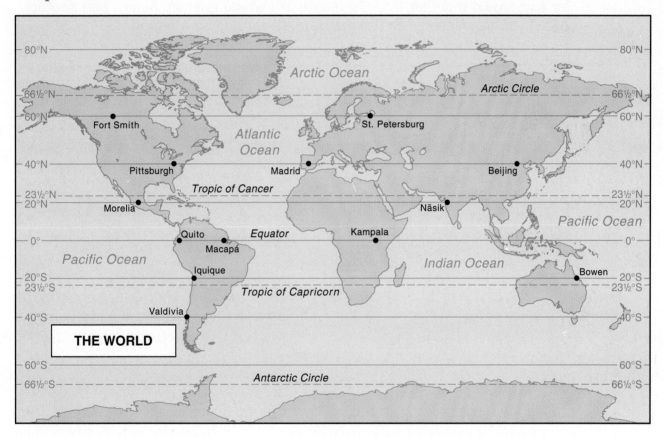

THE WORLD

1. Label the Northern Hemisphere and the Southern Hemisphere on the map above.

2. What is another name for 66½°S latitude? _____

3. What is another name for 23½°N latitude? _____

4. What two cities lie at 60°N? _____

5. What two cities lie at 20°S? _____

6. What two cities lie at 20°N? _____

7. What is the latitude of Quito? _____

Geography Themes Up Close

Regions describes places that share one or more features. A region can be called physical because it is marked by a physical feature, such as climate. The Great Plains is a physical region of the United States that has grasslands as its common feature. A region can be called a human region if it is marked by a human feature, such as language.

The map shows the major urban centers in the United States and Canada. Each center is made up of several large cities and their suburbs that have increased in size and grown together. You can hardly tell where one city begins and another ends. Each urban center on the map can be considered a region.

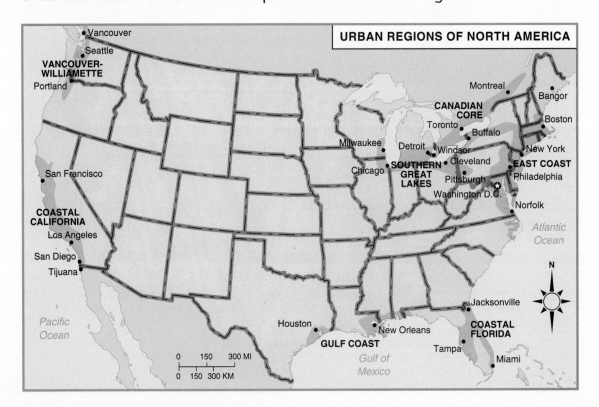

1. What is similar about the location of each urban region in North America?

   _____

2. Use a ruler and the map scale. How many miles long is the Coastal California urban region?

   _____

3. What cities make up the Vancouver-Willamette urban region?

   _____

Regions can be as large as a hemisphere or as small as a neighborhood. The map shows neighborhoods in New Orleans that can be considered regions.

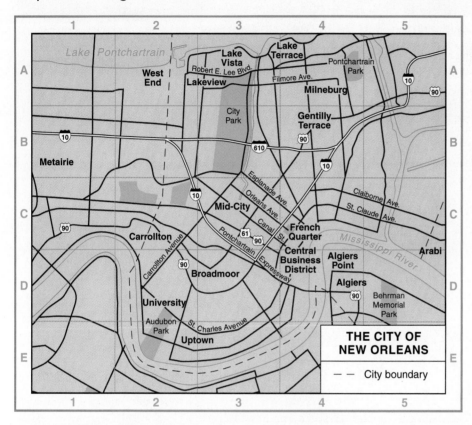

4. The Garden District is found in grid square D-3. This region has many old mansions and beautiful gardens. Label Garden District on the map.

5. What feature do you think the neighborhood called Lakeview has in common?

_____

6. What special features would you expect to find in the French Quarter?

_____

_____

7. How could these neighborhood regions help the government of New Orleans organize the city?

_____

_____

_____

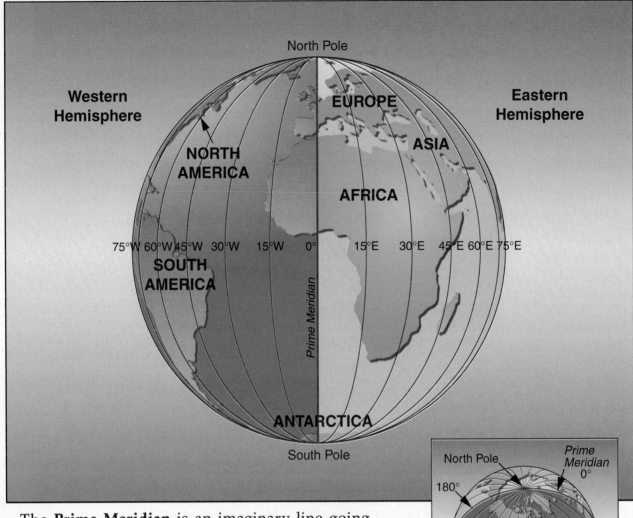

North Pole

Western Hemisphere

Eastern Hemisphere

EUROPE

ASIA

NORTH AMERICA

AFRICA

75°W 60°W 45°W 30°W 15°W 0° 15°E 30°E 45°E 60°E 75°E

SOUTH AMERICA

Prime Meridian

ANTARCTICA

South Pole

North Pole

Prime Meridian 0°

180°

The **Prime Meridian** is an imaginary line going from the North Pole to the South Pole. The Prime Meridian is a line of **longitude**. It is marked 0°. The other lines of longitude measure distance on a globe east and west of the Prime Meridian. All lines of longitude meet at the North and South Poles. Lines of longitude are also called **meridians**.

The 180° meridian and the Prime Meridian form a circle around the globe. That circle divides the globe into two hemispheres. The hemisphere east of the Prime Meridian is the **Eastern Hemisphere**. The hemisphere west of the Prime Meridian is the **Western Hemisphere**.

► Find the Prime Meridian on the large globe above. What continents does it cross?

► What continents and oceans are in the Eastern Hemisphere?

► What continents and oceans are in the Western Hemisphere?

► Find the 45°West meridian. What continents does it cross?

► Find the 45°East meridian. What continents does it cross?

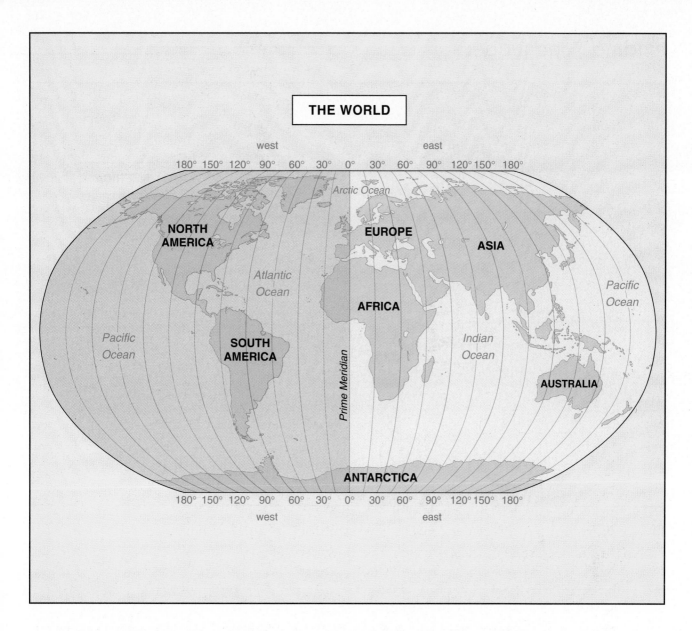

THE WORLD

Lines of longitude are measured in degrees. The Prime Meridian is 0°. All other meridians are numbered east and west of the Prime Meridian up to 180°. The meridians in the Eastern Hemisphere are marked with an *E*. The meridians in the Western Hemisphere are marked with a *W*.

► Find the Prime Meridian on the map.
What oceans does it cross?

► Find the 180° meridian on each side of the map.
Even though you see it twice, it is really the same line.
What oceans does the 180° meridian cross?

► Find the 30°E meridian.
What continents does the 30°E meridian cross?

► Find the 60°W meridian.
What continents does the 60°W meridian cross?

► Why do the meridians curve?

Finding Longitude

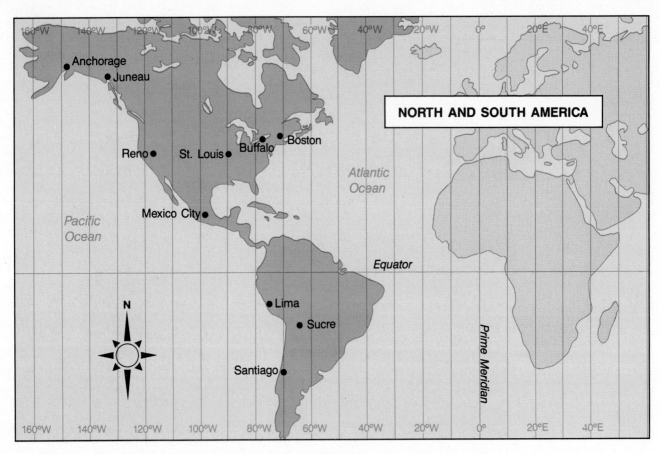

1. Are North and South America east or west of the Prime Meridian? _____
2. North and South America are in which hemisphere?

   _____

3. Trace the 150°W meridian in green.

   What city is near 150°W? _____
4. Trace the 120°W meridian in red.

   What city is near 120°W? _____
5. Trace the 80°W meridian in orange.

   What city is nearest 80°W? _____
6. Find Lima in South America. Circle it.

   Estimate the longitude of Lima. _____
7. Find Sucre in South America. Circle it.

   Estimate the longitude of Sucre. _____
8. Find Juneau in North America. Circle it.

   Estimate the longitude of Juneau. _____

9. What city is north of the Equator and near 70°W longitude? _____

Finding Longitude

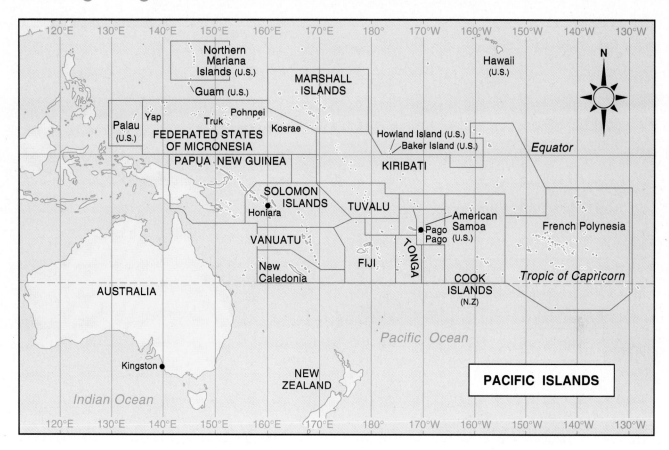

1. Trace the 180° meridian in red.
2. Are the Northern Mariana Islands in the Eastern Hemisphere or Western

   Hemisphere? _____

3. Is American Samoa in the Eastern Hemisphere or Western Hemisphere?

   _____

4. What city is at 160°E? _____

5. In the Federated States of Micronesia, what island is at 138°E? _____

6. What U.S. island lies between 120°E and 140°E? _____

7. What is the longitude of Kingston, Australia? _____

8. Estimate the longitude of Pago Pago. _____

9. Estimate the longitude of Guam. _____

10. Estimate the longitude of Hawaii. _____
11. What two islands are just north of the Equator and at about 176°W?

   _____

Finding Latitude and Longitude

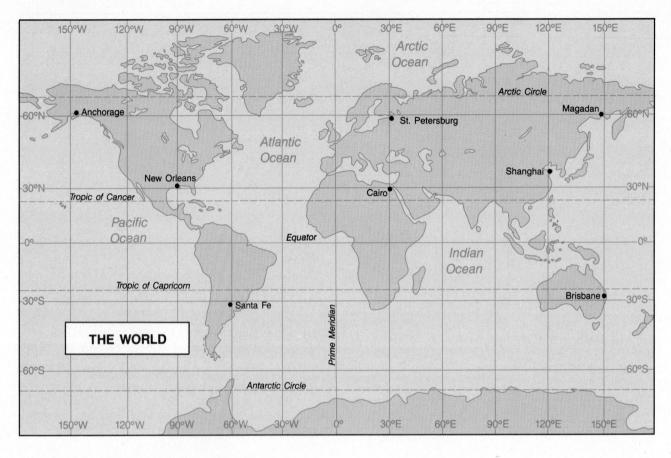

1. Trace the Equator in green.
2. Trace the Prime Meridian in red.
3. Circle the point where the Equator and the Prime Meridian cross.

   Is that point on land or on water? _____
4. Trace the 30°N latitude line in blue.
5. Trace the 90°W longitude line in orange.

6. What city is near the point where 30°N and 90°W cross? _____
7. Trace the 150°E longitude line in purple.
   What two cities lie near this line?

   a. _____   b. _____
8. To locate these cities, you also need to know their degrees latitude.
   Write their degrees latitude after their names in number 7.

9. Anchorage and St. Petersburg are near the same line of latitude.

   What is the line of latitude? _____

10. Anchorage and St. Petersburg are on different lines of longitude. Estimate
    their degrees longitude.

    Anchorage _____   St. Petersburg _____

Skill Check

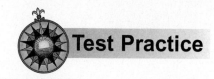
Vocabulary Check

Prime Meridian   longitude   meridian
Eastern Hemisphere   Western Hemisphere

1. Another word for a line of longitude is a _____.

2. The 0° longitude line is also called the _____.

3. The Prime Meridian and the 180° meridian divide the globe into the

_____ and the _____.

Map Check

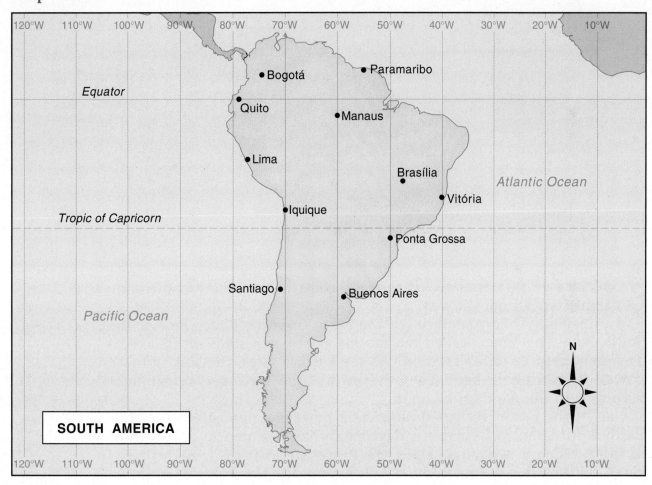

1. Is South America in the Eastern Hemisphere or the Western Hemisphere?

_____

2. What city lies at 40°W? _____

3. Estimate the longitude of Paramaribo. _____

4. What city is south of the Tropic of Capricorn and near 70°W longitude?

_____

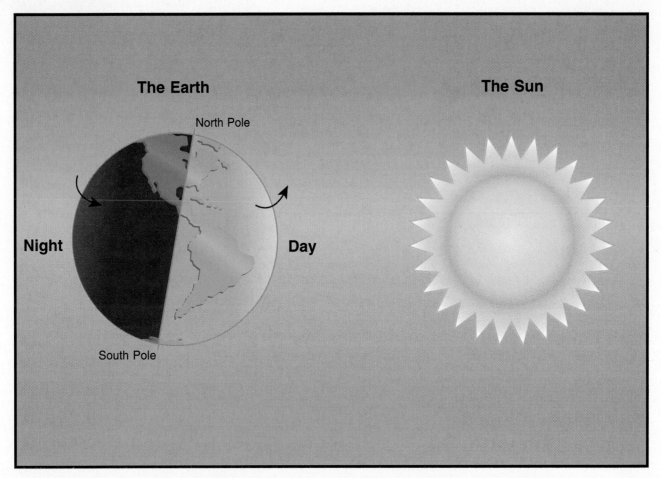

The Earth

The Sun

North Pole

Night

Day

South Pole

Look at the diagram above. It shows the Earth in relation to the sun. Our light comes from the sun.

An imaginary line goes through the Earth from the North Pole to the South Pole. This line is called the Earth's **axis**. Earth spins on its axis. This movement is called **rotation**. As the Earth rotates, the sun shines on part of it, making daylight. The other part of the Earth gets no sunlight, leaving it in the darkness of night.

Half of the Earth receives sunlight at a time. The opposite half of the Earth is in darkness. When it is daytime in North America, it is nighttime in India. When it is daytime along the Prime Meridian, it is nighttime along the 180° line of longitude, which is opposite the Prime Meridian.

Notice that the Earth is tilted. Areas along the Equator always get about the same amount of sunshine, winter or summer. At the North and South Poles, the amount of sunshine changes with the seasons. For a short time during the year, one pole gets sunshine all 24 hours every day. During this same time, the other pole gets no sunshine.

► If it is day in Europe, is it night or day in Australia?

► If it is day in one place on the Equator, is it day everywhere else on the Equator?

► Who sees the sun first, people in New York or people in California?

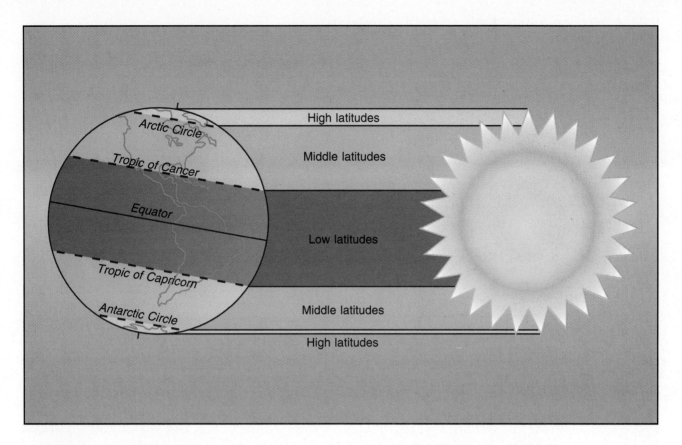

Because the Earth is round, the sun's rays reach the Earth in different ways. The rays are strongest and most direct at the Equator. But at the poles the rays are less strong and direct. Because of this, the Earth is divided into three **climate zones**. **Climate** is the average weather of one place over a long period of time.

Look at the diagram. The area between the Tropic of Capricorn and the Tropic of Cancer receives most of the sun's heat. This climate zone is called the **low latitudes**. Remember that the Equator is 0°. The latitudes close to the Equator have low latitude numbers. Generally the low latitudes have a warm climate.

Look at the areas near the North Pole and the South Pole. These areas receive the least of the sun's heat. They are called the **high latitudes**. The high latitudes are north of the Arctic Circle and south of the Antarctic Circle. Remember that the North and South Poles have the highest latitude numbers—90°. The climate of the high latitudes is usually cold.

Between the high and low latitudes are the **middle latitudes**. The middle latitudes fall between the Tropic of Cancer and the Arctic Circle, and between the Tropic of Capricorn and the Antarctic Circle. The middle latitudes are usually warm in summer and cool in winter.

▶ Find the high latitudes on the diagram.
What continents are in the high latitudes?

▶ Find the middle latitudes on the diagram.
What continents are in the middle latitudes?

▶ Find the low latitudes on the diagram.
What continents are in the low latitudes?

Finish this diagram.

1. Label the sun.
2. Label the Equator.
3. Label the Tropic of Cancer and the Tropic of Capricorn.
4. Label the Arctic Circle and the Antarctic Circle.
5. Label the North Pole and the South Pole.
6. Color the low latitudes red.
7. Color the middle latitudes orange.
8. Color the high latitudes yellow.

9. The North and South Poles are in which climate zone? _____

10. The Equator is in which climate zone? _____

Locating Temperature Zones

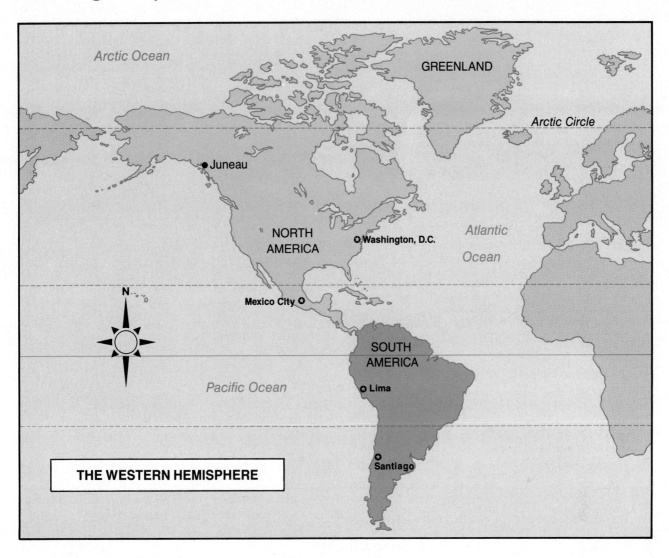

1. Label the Equator.
2. Label the Tropic of Cancer and the Tropic of Capricorn.

3. Greenland is mostly in what climate zone? _____

4. North America is in what three climate zones? _____

_____ and _____

5. Most of North America is in which climate zone? _____

6. Name two cities in the low latitudes. _____

7. Draw a conclusion. Do you think the climate would be warmer in the northern part of South America or in the southern part of South

America? _____

Why? _____

Reading a Climate Map

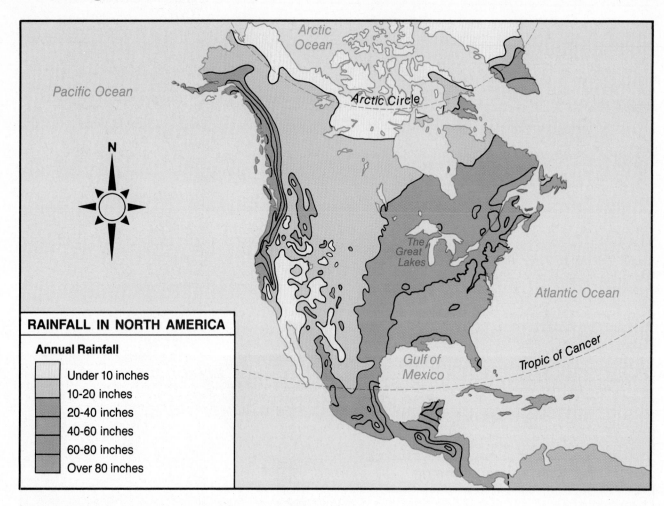

RAINFALL IN NORTH AMERICA

Annual Rainfall

- Under 10 inches
- 10-20 inches
- 20-40 inches
- 40-60 inches
- 60-80 inches
- Over 80 inches

1. Trace the Tropic of Cancer in green.

2. Is there more rain north or south of the Tropic of Cancer? _____

3. What climate zone is just south of the Tropic of Cancer? _____

4. Would the weather there be warm and rainy or cold and rainy?

   _____

5. Trace the Arctic Circle in red.

6. Is there more rain north or south of the Arctic Circle? _____

7. What climate zone is north of the Arctic Circle? _____

8. Would the weather there be cold and wet or cold and dry?

   _____

9. Draw a conclusion. Which latitudes in North America would be better

   for growing food, the high latitudes or the low latitudes? _____

   Why? _____

Skill Check

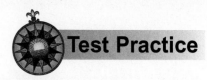

Vocabulary Check   axis   rotation   middle latitudes   climate zone
                         climate   low latitudes   high latitudes

1. The average weather of one place over a long period of time is called

   _____.

2. The Earth spins on its _____.
3. The climate zone south of the Antarctic Circle is called the

   _____.

4. The climate zone between the Tropic of Cancer and the Tropic of

   Capricorn is called the _____.
5. The climate zone between the Tropic of Cancer and the Arctic Circle

   is called the _____.

Map Check

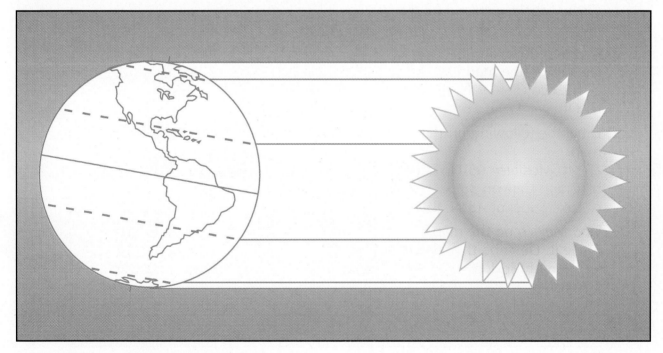

1. Color the high latitudes yellow.
2. Color the middle latitudes orange.
3. Color the low latitudes red.

4. North America is mostly in the _____.

5. The Equator is in the _____.

6. Which climate zone has the coldest weather? _____

Geography Themes Up Close

Location tells where something is found. Every place on Earth has a location. There are two ways of naming a location. **Relative location** tells what it is near or what is around it. **Absolute location** gives the exact location by using latitude and longitude lines.

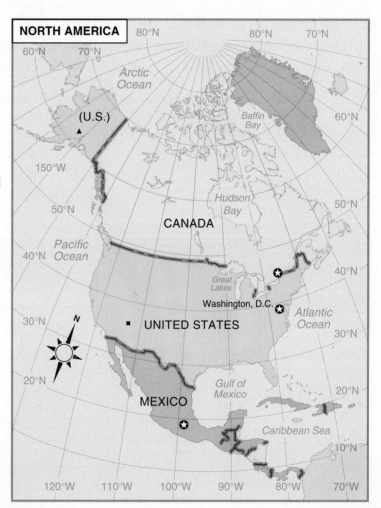

1. Greenland, the largest island in the world, is located northeast of Canada. Greenland is located east of Baffin Bay. Most of Greenland is north of the Arctic Circle. Label Greenland on the map.

2. Label the following national capitals on the map.
   a. Mexico City 19°N, 99°W
   b. Ottawa 45°N, 76°W

3. Label the following on the map.
   a. Mt. McKinley 63°N, 151°W
   b. Grand Canyon 36°N, 112°W
   c. Lake Superior 48°N, 89°W

4. Find Mexico on the map. Circle it. Describe the relative location of Mexico.

_____

_____

_____

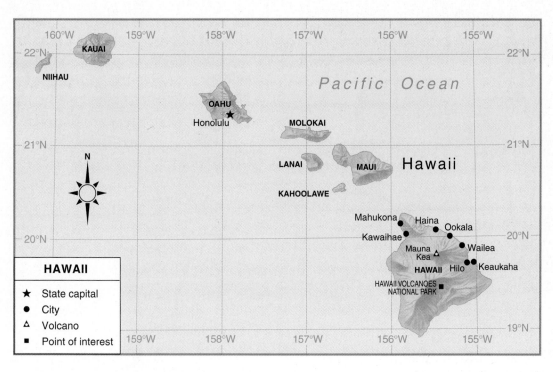

5. Describe the relative location of Honolulu. Explain why its location might be one reason Honolulu was chosen as the capital of Hawaii.

_____

_____

_____

6. What is the absolute location of the volcano Mauna Kea—the highest point in Hawaii?

_____

7. Where are most cities and towns on the island of Hawaii located? Why do you think this is so?

_____

_____

_____

_____

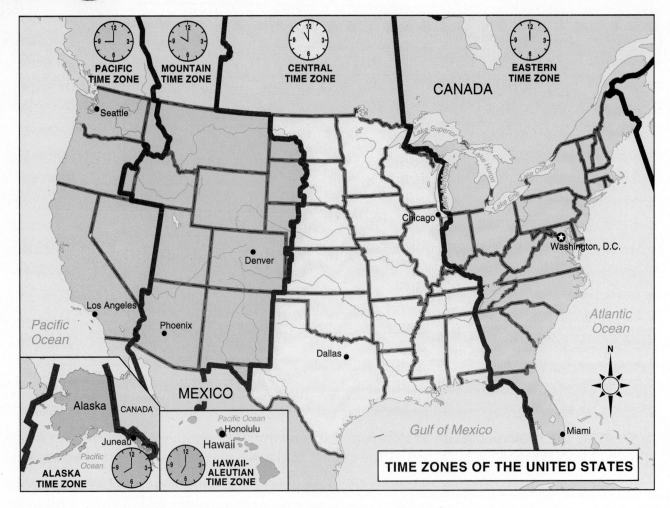

TIME ZONES OF THE UNITED STATES

You know that the Earth is turning all the time. It makes one complete rotation or turn every 24 hours. Remember that the Earth gets its light from the sun. Only half of the Earth receives light at a time. As the Earth turns, one part of the Earth gets lighter while another part gets darker.

It is not the same time everywhere on Earth. The Earth is divided into 24 time zones. There is one time zone for each hour in the day.

Six of the world's 24 **time zones** are in the United States. Look at the time zone map above. The time in each zone is different by one hour from the zone next to it. Washington, D.C. is in the Eastern Time Zone. Chicago is in the Central Time Zone. When it is 8:00 A.M. in Washington, D.C., it is 7:00 A.M. in Chicago. In Denver, which is in the Mountain Time Zone, it is 6:00 A.M. In San Francisco, which is in the Pacific Time Zone, it is 5:00 A.M. In the Alaska Time Zone, it is 4:00 A.M. In the Hawaii-Aleutian Time Zone, it is 3:00 A.M.

► In which time zone do you live?

► How do you think the Pacific Time Zone got its name?

► What mountain range goes through the Mountain Time Zone?

► New York City is in which time zone?

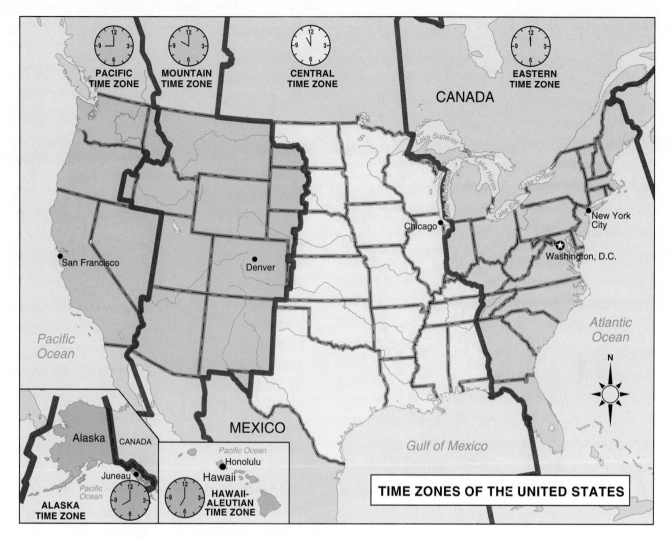

If you know the time in one time zone, you can find the time in others. If you go east one time zone, add one hour to the time. If you go east two time zones, add two hours to the time. If you go west one time zone, subtract one hour from the time.

Look at the time zone map above. Put your finger on the Mountain Time Zone. Suppose it is 7:00 there. Move your finger one time zone east, to the Central Time Zone. Add one hour to the time. It is 8:00 Central time.

Move your finger back to the Mountain Time Zone. It is still 7:00. Now move your finger one time zone west to the Pacific Time Zone. Remember, you subtract one hour for each time zone you go west.

► What time is it in the Pacific Time Zone?

► Name two cities in each time zone.

► If it is 6:00 in Chicago, what time is it in Washington, D.C.?
What time is it in Phoenix?
What time is it in Seattle?

► If it is 12:00 noon in Chicago, what time is it in Washington, D.C.?
What time is it in Honolulu?
What time is it in Juneau?

Reading a Time Zone Map

1. Lightly color the time zones. Use a different color for each zone. Notice that the lines are not always straight. Time zones often follow state boundaries or physical features.

2. In which time zone do you find these states?

California _____   Pennsylvania _____

Illinois _____   Hawaii _____

3. It is 10:00 A.M. in California. What time is it in Wyoming? _____

4. It is 5:00 P.M. in Georgia. What time is it in Alaska? _____

5. It is 12:00 noon in Illinois. What time is it in Virginia? _____

6. It is 4:00 P.M. in Massachusetts. What time is it in Oklahoma? _____

7. It is 12:00 midnight in Iowa. What time is it in New Mexico? _____

8. It is 4:30 A.M. in Colorado. What time is it in Washington state? _____

Reading a Time Zone Map

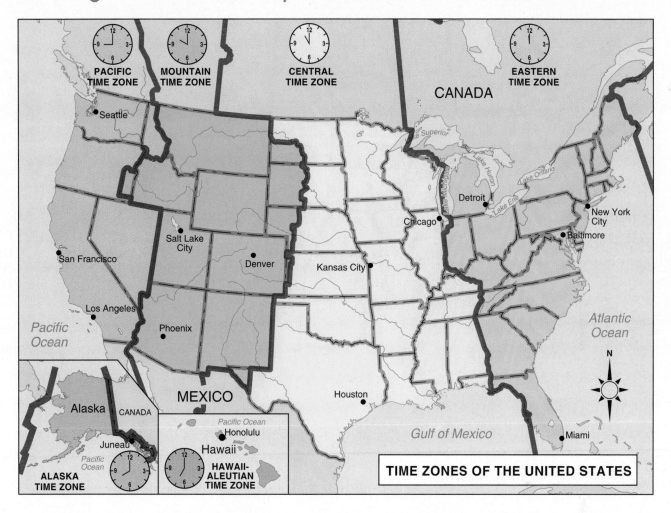

1. It is 7:00 A.M. in Denver. What time is it in the cities listed below?

   Honolulu _____   Phoenix _____

   Los Angeles _____   Miami _____

   Detroit _____   New York City _____

2. It is 12:00 noon in Chicago. What time is it in the cities listed below?

   Juneau _____   Seattle _____

   Denver _____   Baltimore _____

   Houston _____   San Francisco _____

3. The first people to see the sunrise live in the _____ Time Zone.

4. The last people to see the sun set live in the _____ Time Zone.

Reading a Time Zone Map

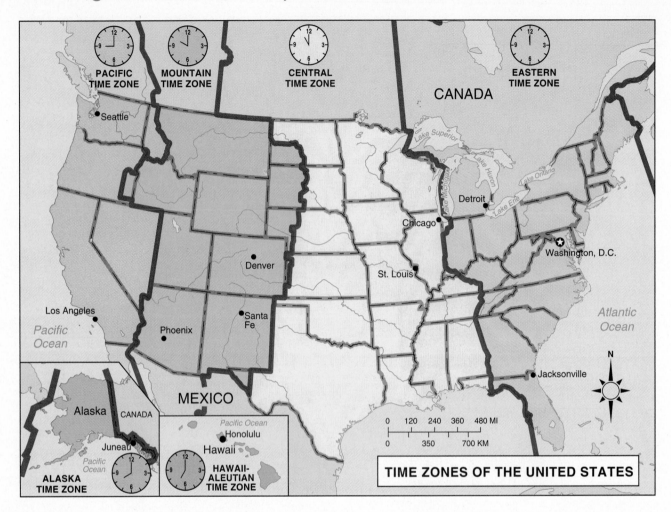

1. You will be traveling to several cities in the United States. Draw a line from

   Jacksonville to St. Louis. What direction will you be traveling? _____
   When you arrive in St. Louis, it is 2:00 P.M. What time is it in

   Jacksonville? _____

2. From St. Louis, you will drive to Denver. Draw a line to connect these

   two cities. From St. Louis to Denver is about _____ miles. What

   direction will you be traveling? _____

3. You will drive from Denver to Los Angeles to visit friends. Draw a line
   connecting these two cities.

   It is 7:00 A.M. in Los Angeles. What time is it in Denver? _____

   What time is it in Jacksonville? _____

Skill Check

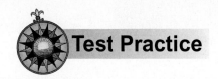

Vocabulary Check   time zone

Map Check

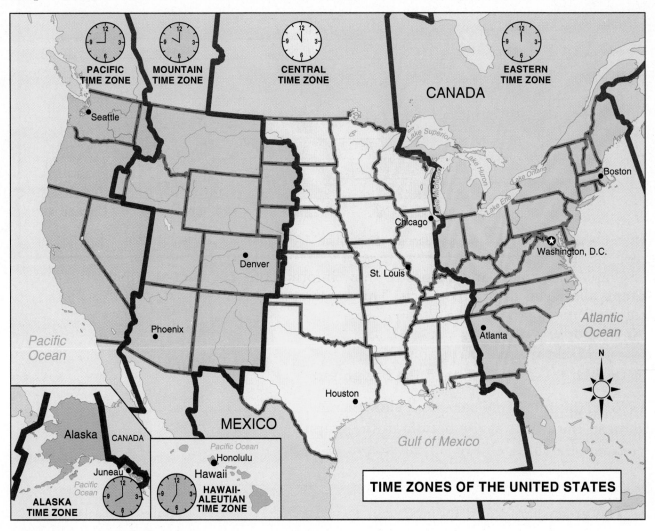

TIME ZONES OF THE UNITED STATES

1. The Earth is divided into 24 _____.

2. Atlanta is in the _____ Time Zone.

3. Phoenix is in the _____ Time Zone.

4. It is 2:00 P.M. in St. Louis. What time is it in the following cities?

   Denver _____   Seattle _____

   Atlanta _____   Honolulu _____

5. It is 12:00 noon in Denver. What time is it in the following cities?

   Houston _____   Seattle _____

   Juneau _____   Washington, D.C. _____

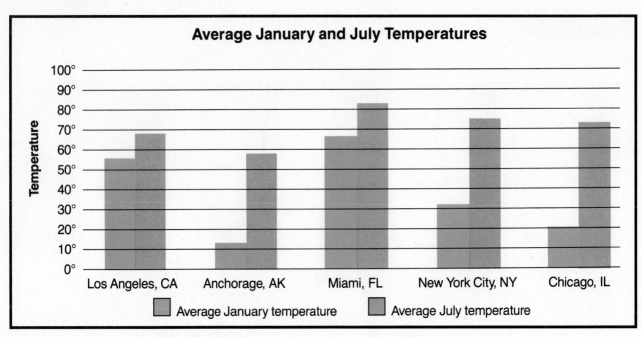

Average January and July Temperatures

■ Average January temperature ■ Average July temperature

Graphs use colors and shapes to show information. The bars on a **bar graph** allow you to compare facts. This bar graph shows two temperatures for five cities.

GRAPH ATTACK!

Follow these steps to read the bar graph.

1. Read the title. This bar graph shows _____.
2. Read the words at the bottom of the graph.
   Name the cities shown on the graph.

   _____

   The green bars stand for _____.

   The orange bars stand for _____.
3. Read the words and numbers on the left side of the graph. The

   numbers on the graph stand for _____.
4. Compare the bars. Put your finger at the top of the first bar for Miami.
   Slide your finger to the left. Read the number there.

   The average January temperature in Miami is about _____.

   The average July temperature in Miami is about _____.

   Which city has the lowest January temperature? _____.
5. Draw a conclusion. Which three cities have the coldest winters?

   _____

Reading a Bar Graph

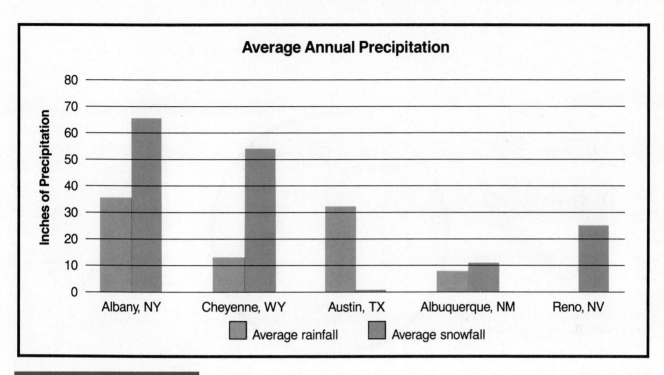

Average Annual Precipitation

Inches of Precipitation

Albany, NY | Cheyenne, WY | Austin, TX | Albuquerque, NM | Reno, NV

☐ Average rainfall ☐ Average snowfall

GRAPH ATTACK!

Follow these steps to read the bar graph.

1. Read the title. This bar graph shows _____.
2. Read the words at the bottom of the graph.

   The brown bars on this graph stand for _____.

   The blue bars on this graph stand for _____.
3. Read the words and numbers at the left side of the graph.

   The numbers on the graph stand for _____.
4. Compare the bars. Use more or less in each sentence.

   Cheyenne receives _____ snow than Albany.

   Austin receives _____ rain than Albuquerque.

   Reno receives _____ snow than Albuquerque.

   Which city receives the most rain? _____

   Which city receives the least snow? _____
5. Finish the graph. Reno, Nevada receives 8 inches of rain. Add a bar showing the amount of rain Reno receives.
6. Draw a conclusion. Which city gets about the same amount of rain

   as snow? _____

Circle Graphs

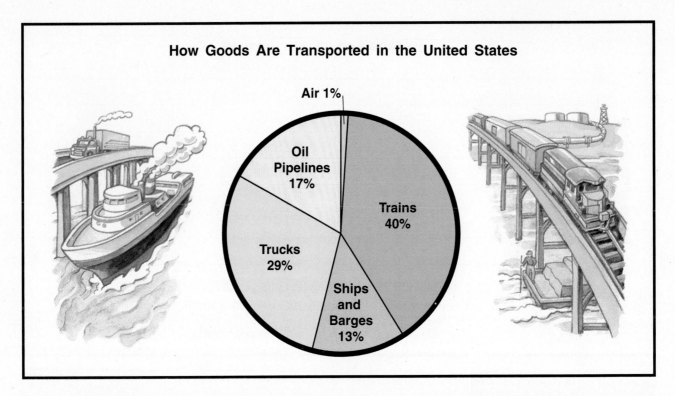

How Goods Are Transported in the United States

Air 1%

Oil Pipelines 17%

Trains 40%

Trucks 29%

Ships and Barges 13%

A **circle graph** shows the parts that make up a whole set of facts. Each part of the circle is a percentage of the whole. All the parts together equal 100%. This circle graph shows the percentage of all goods moved by each method of transportation.

GRAPH ATTACK!

Follow these steps to read the circle graph.

1. <u>Read the title.</u> The whole circle shows _____

   _____.

2. <u>Read each part of the circle.</u> Each part of the circle stands for a different way of transporting goods. What are the different ways?

   _____

3. <u>Compare the parts.</u> Read clockwise around the circle from the biggest part. Write <u>More</u> or <u>Fewer</u> in each sentence.

   _____ goods are carried by trucks than by ships and barges.

   _____ goods are carried by trucks than by trains.

   _____ goods are carried by trains than by oil pipelines and ships and barges together.

4. <u>Draw a conclusion.</u> What two methods of transportation carry about the same amount of goods? _____

Reading a Circle Graph

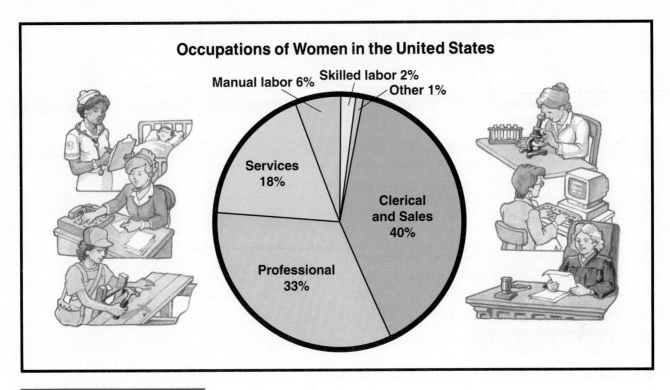

Occupations of Women in the United States

Manual labor 6% Skilled labor 2%
Other 1%
Services 18%
Clerical and Sales 40%
Professional 33%

GRAPH ATTACK!

Follow these steps to read the circle graph.

1. <u>Read the title.</u> The circle graph shows _____
2. <u>Read each part of the circle.</u>

   What percent of women hold clerical and sales positions? _____

   What percent of women hold manual labor positions? _____

   What percent of women hold positions in manual and skilled labor? _____
3. <u>Compare the parts of the circle.</u> Use <u>More</u> or <u>Fewer</u> in each sentence.

   _____ women hold positions in skilled labor than in manual labor.

   _____ women hold professional positions than clerical and sales positions.

   _____ women hold professional positions than clerical and sales positions.

   Would you be more likely to meet a woman who was a professional or a woman who was in services? _____

4. <u>Draw a conclusion.</u> Most women work in what three areas?

   _____

Line Graphs

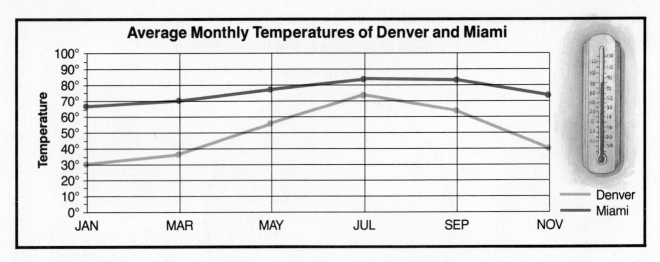

Average Monthly Temperatures of Denver and Miami

Denver
Miami

Some students wanted to compare the climate of two U.S. cities. They made a line graph to show the temperatures of these two cities. A **line graph** shows how something changes over time.

GRAPH ATTACK!

Follow these steps to read a line graph.

1. Read the title. This line graph shows _____

_____.

2. Read the words along the bottom of the graph.
This line graph shows the average temperatures for the months of

_____.

3. Read the words and numbers on the left side of the graph. These numbers

stand for _____. The highest number is _____.

4. Read the lines on the graph.
Find the line for Miami. Put your finger on the dot above January.
Slide your finger to the left and read the temperature.

In January the average temperature in Miami is about _____.

In January the average temperature in Denver is _____.

5. Compare the lines.

Which city has the hottest summer temperatures? _____

Which city has the coldest temperatures? _____

6. Draw a conclusion.

Which city's temperatures change the least over the year? _____

How do you know? _____

Reading a Line Graph

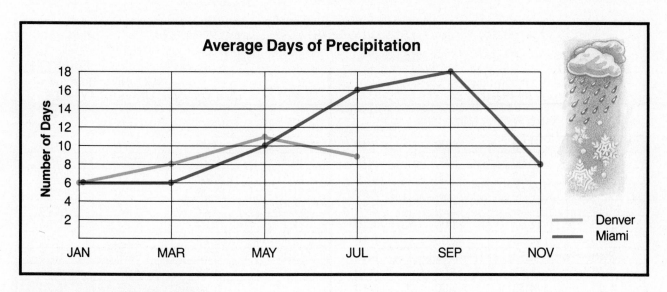

Average Days of Precipitation

Denver
Miami

GRAPH ATTACK!

Follow the first three steps on page 88 to begin reading this line graph.

1. Trace the line for Miami with your finger. Put your finger at the highest point on the line.

   What month does the dot stand for? _____

   How many days of precipitation did Miami have in that month? _____

   How many days of precipitation did Miami have in May? _____
   In what two months did Miami have the same number of days of

   precipitation? _____

2. Finish the graph. Finish the line for Denver. Add dots for this information. Then complete the line.

   September 5 days   November 5 days

3. Compare the lines.

   Which city had more days of precipitation in July? _____

   Which city had more days of precipitation in May? _____

   Which city had fewer days of precipitation in November? _____
   In what month did Miami and Denver have the same number of days of

   precipitation? _____

4. Draw a conclusion. Which city had the biggest change in number of days of

   precipitation overall? _____ How do you know? _____

   _____

| University Hills Bus Schedule WEEKDAY & SATURDAY SERVICE | | | | | | | |
| OUTBOUND from downtown (Bus sign reads AIRPORT) | | | | INBOUND to downtown (Bus sign reads UNIVERSITY HILLS) | | | |
5th & Congress	9th & Park	12th & Park	Airport & River Road	12th & Park	9th & Park	9th & Capitol	5th & Capitol
7:45	7:53	8:00	8:10	8:17	8:22	8:27	8:35
8:45	8:53	9:00	9:10	9:17	9:22	9:27	9:35
9:45	9:53	10:00	10:10	10:17	10:22	10:27	10:35
10:45	10:53	11:00	11:10	11:17	11:22	11:27	11:35
11:45	11:53	12:00	12:10	12:17	12:22	12:27	12:35
12:45	12:53	1:00	1:10	1:17	1:22	1:27	1:35
1:45	1:53	2:00	2:10	2:17	2:22	2:27	2:35
2:45	2:53	3:00	3:10	3:17	3:22	3:27	3:35
3:45	3:53	4:00	4:10	4:17	4:22	4:27	4:35
4:45	4:53	5:00	5:10	5:17	5:22	5:27	5:35

A **table** shows information using rows and columns. Tables put a large amount of information in a small space. This table is a bus schedule.

TABLE ATTACK!

Follow these steps to read the table.

1. Read the title. This table shows the _____.
2. Read the words at the top of the table.

Where is the first stop? _____

When the bus is outbound, what does the bus sign read? _____

What do the numbers in each column stand for? _____

On what day could you not ride this bus? _____

3. Read the table. If you caught the bus at 5th and Congress at 9:45,

what time would you get to Airport and River Road? _____
If you caught the bus at 12th and Park at 2:17, what time would you

get to 9th and Capitol? _____
If you needed to be at the airport at 12:30, what time should you catch

the bus at 5th and Congress? _____
If your plane arrived at 2:00, what is the earliest you could arrive at

5th and Capitol? _____
4. Draw a conclusion. Where does the bus make a loop and head back

toward downtown? _____

Reading a Table

| Road Mileages Between U.S. Cities | | | | | | | |
Cities	Birmingham	Boston	Buffalo	Chicago	Cleveland	Dallas	Denver
Boston, MA	1,215	—	461	1,003	654	1,819	2,004
Chicago, IL	667	1,003	545	—	346	936	1,015
Dallas, TX	647	1,819	1,393	936	1,208	—	887
Denver, CO	1,356	2,004	1,546	1,015	1,347	887	—
Detroit, MI	734	751		283	171	1,218	1,284
Kansas City, MO	753	1,427	995	532	806	554	603
Los Angeles, CA	2,092		2,512	2,042	2,374	1,446	1,029
Miami, FL	812	1,529	1,425	1,382	1,250	1,367	2,069
Minneapolis, MN	1,079	1,417	958	409	760	999	924
New Orleans, LA	351	1,563	1,254	935	1,070		1,409
New York, NY	985	215	400	797	466	1,589	1,799
Philadelphia, PA	897	321	414	768	437	1,501	1,744
Salt Lake City, UT	1,868	2,395	1,936	1,406	1,738	1,410	531
San Francisco, CA	2,472	3,135	2,677	2,146	2,478	1,827	1,271
Washington, DC	758	458	384	695	370	1,362	1,686

TABLE ATTACK!

Follow these steps to read the table.

1. <u>Read the title.</u>

   This table shows _____.

2. <u>Read the words at the top of the table.</u> What cities are listed across the

   top? _____

3. <u>Read the words at the left of the table.</u> How many cities are listed? ____

4. <u>Read the table.</u> Put your finger on Boston at the left of the table. Slide your finger to the right until you come to the number under Chicago. Read that number.

   The distance from Boston to Chicago is _____ miles.

5. <u>Finish the table.</u> Add these distances.

   Detroit to Buffalo   277 miles
   Los Angeles to Boston   3,046 miles
   New Orleans to Dallas 525 miles

6. <u>Draw a conclusion.</u> Which of the cities listed is farthest from Dallas?

   _____

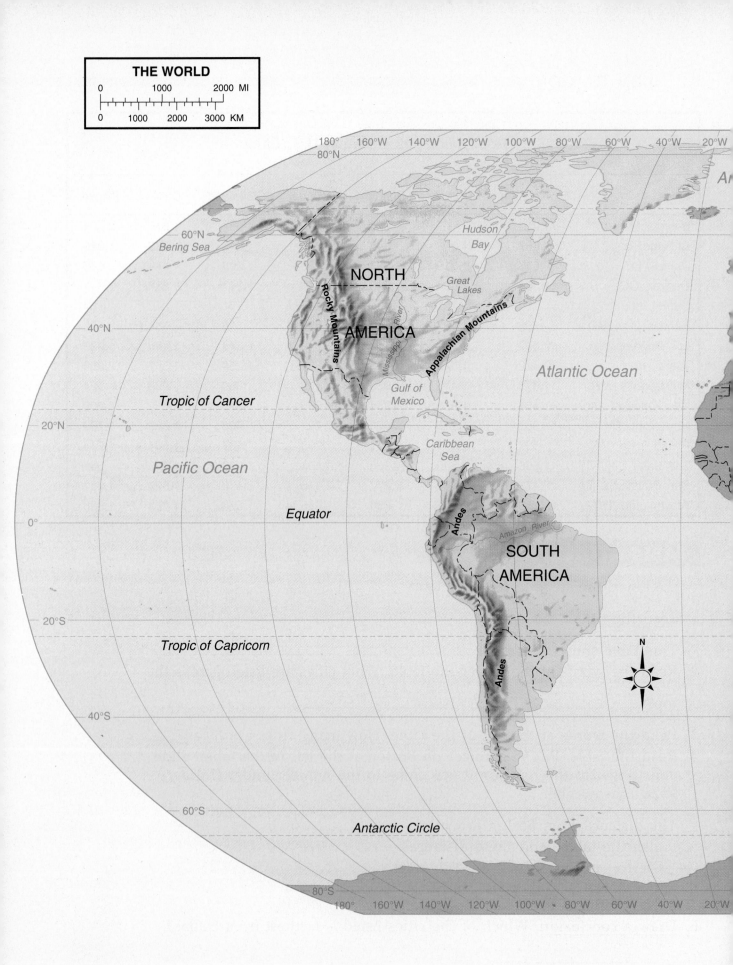

THE WORLD

0   1000   2000 MI

0   1000   2000   3000 KM

80°N

180°   160°W   140°W   120°W   100°W   80°W   60°W   40°W   20°W

60°N
Bering Sea

Hudson
Bay

NORTH

Great
Lakes

Rocky Mountains

40°N

Mississippi River

AMERICA

Appalachian Mountains

Atlantic Ocean

Tropic of Cancer

Gulf of
Mexico

20°N

Caribbean
Sea

Pacific Ocean

Andes

Equator

0°

Amazon River

SOUTH

AMERICA

N

20°S

Tropic of Capricorn

Andes

40°S

60°S

Antarctic Circle

80°S

180°   160°W   140°W   120°W   100°W   80°W   60°W   40°W   20°W

20°E 40°E 60°E 80°E 100°E 120°E 140°E 160°E 180°

cean

80°N

Arctic Circle

60°N

Ural Mountains

Volga River

Ob

River

ASIA

EUROPE

Danube

s

River

Black Sea

Caspian Sea

40°N

Mediterranean Sea

The Himalaya

s

Red Sea

Ganges River

River

20°N

AFRICA

Nile

Arabian
Sea

Pacific Ocean

Congo River

0°

Indian Ocean

20°S

AUSTRALIA

Great Dividing Range

40°S

60°S

ANTARCTICA

80°S

20°E 40°E 60°E 80°E 100°E 120°E 140°E 160°E 180°

THE UNITED STATES

International Boundary

State Boundary

☆ National Capital

★ State Capital

500 MI
0 100 200 300 400 500

800 KM
0 100 200 300 400 500 600 700 800

CANADA

RUSSIA

Maine · Augusta

New Hampshire · Concord

Massachusetts · Boston

Vermont · Montpelier

New York · Albany

Rhode Island · Providence

Connecticut · Hartford

New Jersey · Trenton

Delaware · Dover

Washington, D.C.

Maryland · Annapolis

Pennsylvania · Harrisburg

West Virginia · Charleston

Virginia · Richmond

North Carolina · Raleigh

South Carolina · Columbia

Ohio · Columbus

Kentucky · Frankfort

Tennessee · Nashville

Georgia · Atlanta

Alabama · Montgomery

Florida · Tallahassee

Michigan · Lansing

Indiana · Indianapolis

Illinois · Springfield

Missouri · Jefferson City

Arkansas · Little Rock

Mississippi · Jackson

Louisiana · Baton Rouge

Wisconsin · Madison

Iowa · Des Moines

Minnesota · St. Paul

North Dakota · Bismarck

South Dakota · Pierre

Nebraska · Lincoln

Kansas · Topeka

Oklahoma · Oklahoma City

Texas · Austin

Colorado · Denver

Wyoming · Cheyenne

New Mexico · Santa Fe

Montana · Helena

Idaho · Boise

Utah · Salt Lake City

Arizona · Phoenix

Washington · Olympia

Oregon · Salem

Nevada · Carson City

California · Sacramento

Appalachian Mountains

Rocky Mountains

Sierra Nevada

Cascade Range

Atlantic Ocean

Pacific Ocean

Gulf of Mexico

MEXICO

Lake Superior

Lake Michigan

Lake Huron

Lake Erie

Lake Ontario

Lake Okeechobee

Mississippi River

Ohio River

Missouri River

Red River

Minnesota River

Arkansas River

Brazos River

Rio Grande

Colorado River

Snake River

Columbia River

Great Salt Lake

Alaska · Juneau

CANADA

Arctic Ocean

Yukon River

400 MI
0 200 400 KM

Hawaii · Honolulu

100 MI
0 50 100 KM

Pacific Ocean

Glossary

absolute location (p. 76)   the specific address or latitude and longitude coordinates of a place

acid rain (p. 48)   a kind of pollution that people cause that mixes with water vapor and falls to the ground as damaging rain or snow

Antarctic Circle (p. 57)   the parallel of latitude 66½° south of the Equator

Arctic Circle (p. 57)   the parallel of latitude 66½° north of the Equator

axis (p. 70)   the imaginary line that goes through Earth from the North Pole to the South Pole. Earth spins on its axis.

bar graph (p. 84)   a graph that uses thick bars of different lengths to compare numbers or amounts

cardinal directions (p. 8)   north, south, east, and west

charts (p. 35)   facts shown in columns and rows

circle graph (p. 86)   a graph that shows how something whole is divided into parts

climate (p. 71)   the average weather of a place over a long period of time

climate zone (p. 71)   an area with a generally similar climate

compass rose (p. 9)   a symbol that shows directions on a map

degrees (p. 56)   the units of latitude and longitude lines

elevation (p. 37)   the height of land above the level of the sea

Equator (p. 56)   the imaginary line around the middle of Earth that divides Earth into the Northern and Southern Hemispheres

geography (p. 4)   the study of Earth, its features, and how people live and work on Earth

grid (p. 50)   a pattern of lines drawn on a map that cross each other to form squares

hemisphere (p. 56)   half of a sphere; half of Earth; the four hemispheres are Eastern, Western, Northern, and Southern

high latitudes (p. 71)   the areas north of the Arctic Circle and south of the Antarctic Circle. These areas receive the least of the sun's heat.

human/environment interaction (pp. 5, 48)   the ways that the environment affects people and people affect the environment

human features (p. 4)   features of a place made by people, such as airports, buildings, highways, businesses, parks, and playgrounds

inset map (p. 23)   a small map within a larger map

interdependence (p. 34)   how people depend on one another to meet their needs and wants

intermediate directions (p. 9)   northeast, southeast, southwest, northwest

international boundary (p. 14)   where one country ends and another begins

interstate highway (p. 28)   a main highway that crosses the entire country

kilometers (p. 22)   a unit of length used in measuring distance in the metric system. Kilometers can also be written **KM** and km.

latitude (p. 56)   the distance north or south of the Equator measured in degrees

legend (p. 14)   a map key, or list of symbols on a map and what they stand for

line graph (p. 88)   a graph that shows how something changes over time

location (pp. 4, 76)   the absolute and relative position of people and places on Earth

longitude (p. 64)   the distance east or west of the Prime Meridian, measured in degrees

low latitudes (p. 71)   the area between the Tropic of Capricorn and Tropic of Cancer, which receives most of the sun's heat

map index (p. 51)   the alphabetical list of places on a map with their grid squares

map scale (p. 22)   the guide that shows what distances on a map equal in the real world

meridians (p. 64)   lines of longitude

middle latitudes (p. 71)   the areas between the Tropic of Cancer and the Arctic Circle and Tropic of Capricorn and the Antarctic Circle. These areas are warm in the summer and cool in winter.

mileage markers (p. 29)   small triangles and numbers on a map used to indicate distances along highways

miles (p. 22)   a unit of length that can also be written **MI** or mi

mountain range (p. 36)   a group or chain of mountains

movement (pp. 6, 34)   how and why people, goods, information, and ideas move from place to place

North Pole (p. 8)   the point farthest north on Earth

parallels (p. 56)   lines of latitude

physical features (p. 4)   natural features of a place, such as climate, landforms, soil, bodies of water, and plants and animals

physical map (p. 37)   a map that shows elevation and relief

place (pp. 4, 20)   physical and human features that make a location different from any other

plain (p. 36)   a large area of flat land

political map (p. 15)   a map that shows the boundaries separating states and countries

population map (p. 43)   a map that shows the number of people living in an area

Prime Meridian (p. 64)   the line of longitude from the North Pole to the South Pole and marked 0°. It helps divide Earth into the Eastern and Western Hemispheres.

regions (pp. 7, 29, 62)   places that share one or more features

relative location (p. 76)   describes a location by telling what it is near or what is around it

relief map (p. 36)   a map that shows the land on Earth

resource map (p. 43)   a map that uses symbols to show things in nature that people can use, such as coal, oil, and gold

rotation (p. 70)   the movement Earth makes as it spins around its axis

route (p. 28)   a road or path from one place to another, such as a trail, highway, railroad, or waterway

scenic road (p. 28)   a road that goes through beautiful areas

sea level (p. 37)   the level of the ocean surface

South Pole (p. 8)   the point farthest south on Earth

special purpose map (p. 42)   a map that gives information about a specific subject, such as climate, people, resources, or history

state boundary (p. 14)   where one state ends and another begins

state highway (p. 28)   a main road that connects cities and towns within the boundaries of one state

symbol (p. 14)   a picture on a map that stands for something real

table (p. 90)   a way of showing a large amount of information in a small space, using rows and columns

temperature map (p. 43)   a map that shows temperatures for an area

themes (p. 4)   main topics

time zone (p. 78)   an area on Earth where the time is the same. Earth is divided into 24 time zones.

title (p. 15)   the name of a map

Tropic of Cancer (p. 57)   the parallel of latitude 23½° north of the Equator

Tropic of Capricorn (p. 57)   the parallel of latitude 23½° south of the Equator